MW00438748

"This is a book you can't
lenges you and never fai   people who
haven't had the privilege of hearing Stan Linzey in person will be
able to read about the tremendous move of the Holy Spirit that
accompanied his military career. Get this book, read this book and
be impacted by a mighty man of God."

Dr. Coleman Phillips
Senior Pastor, Cathedral of the Valley
FourSquare Church, Escondido, CA

"This striking account of my father's pilgrimage – his involvement
in spiritual warfare in the world's greatest naval battle – produced
victories at MIDWAY. This book will impact upon your life."

George W. Linzey
Captain, CHC, USN

"Stan Linzey recounts from personal experience how God miracu-
lously intervened in the Battle Of Midway. His account will
strengthen you faith and encourage you to be open to the leading of
the Holy Spirit for prayer and expectation of supernatural results.
This is must reading."

Harvey J. Beeton
Captain, USN, (Ret.)

"*God Was At Midway* is a remarkably intriguing and compelling
account of the Battles of the Coral Sea and Midway as seen through
the Christian eyes of the Lord's servant, Captain Stanford E.
Linzey, CHC, USN, (Ret.). Dr. Linzey allows the reader to easily
understand and visualize not only the tragedies of combat, but the
human and spiritual elements of surviving the harrowing and horri-
fying disasters of naval warfare."

Dahk Knox, Ph.D., Ed.D., CDR, USNR, (Ret.)
Author and World War II Historian

GOD WAS
AT
MIDWAY

The Sinking of the USS YORKTOWN (CV-5)

and the Battles of the Coral Sea and Midway

BY

Captain Stanford E. Linzey., Chaplain, USN (RET.)

BLACK FOREST PRESS
San Diego, California
August, 1996

First Edition

GOD WAS AT MIDWAY

The Sinking of the USS YORKTOWN (CV-5)
and the Battles of the Coral Sea and Midway

BY

Captain Stanford E. Linzey., Chaplain, USN (RET.)

PUBLISHED IN THE UNITED STATES OF AMERICA
BY
BLACK FOREST PRESS
539 TELEGRAPH CANYON ROAD
BOX 521
CHULA VISTA, CA 91910
(619) 656-8048

Cover Design Dahk Knox
Cover Artwork Jan Lowry

Disclaimer

This document is an original work of the author. It may include reference to information commonly known or freely available to the general public. Any resemblance to other published information is purely coincidental. The author has in no way attempted to use material not of his own origination. Black Forest Press disclaims any association with or responsibility for the ideas, opinions or facts as expressed by the author of this book.

Printed in the United States of America
Library of Congress
Cataloging-in-Publication

ISBN: 1-881116-80-8

Copyright © August 1996 by Captain Stanford E. Linzey, Jr., Chaplain, USN (RET)

ALL RIGHTS RESERVED

DEDICATION

To the brave friends we left behind at the Battle of Midway, to the many family members who have mourned their loss, and to the survivors of the sinking of the USS YORKTOWN who continue to meet annually in memory of that tragic yet victorious day.

CONTENTS

FOREWORD

Dr. Stanford E. Linzey, Jr., is one of our World War II heroes. He survived two major sea battles, two bombings of his ship, and the torpedo attack that sank the Aircraft Carrier USS YORKTOWN at Midway. Even though as a young sailor he felt helpless in the face of such destructive forces, he experienced the effects of the prayers of Christian people in America and heard from God at the very time of the battle.

The Battles of the Coral Sea and Midway stand apart from all others, for they were the first naval battles in history in which the opposing ships did not see one another but attacked with aircraft. Nor will such battles occur again, for the greater range of attack planes and the increasing sophistication of ballistic missiles have made such sea conflicts obsolete.

Although I have known Stan and Verna Linzey for some thirty years, I first heard him tell this war story in the church I pastored in San Jose, California, in the mid-1980's. I encouraged him to write his story and eventually agreed to join him in the project. Few people remember him as an enlisted sailor, but many have known him as a U.S. Navy chaplain and more recently as an evangelist and speaker for his Holy Spirit Seminars. He is the author of **Pentecost in the Pentagon** and often speaks for meetings of the Full Gospel Businessmen's Fellowship. A dedicated and outspoken Pentecostal, he has led thousands of believers to experience the baptism in the Holy Spirit and is in constant demand as a speaker.

After his heroic participation in several great battles of World War II, Stan Linzey pastored churches in California while pursuing his education and eventually became a U.S. Navy chaplain. Over the years, he served in many different ships and posts and is best remembered as Command Chaplain of the aircraft carrier USS CORAL SEA. At retirement, he held the rank of captain (USN) and was the highest ranking naval officer in the Assemblies of God. He earned his doctorate in Theology at Fuller Theological Seminary in 1980.

Stan Linzey served with distinction both as a seaman, for eight years during World War II, and as a chaplain for twenty years after the Korean War.

Chaplain Lemuel D. McElyea, Colonel, USAF (Ret.), who serves as national secretary of the Assemblies of God Chaplaincy Department and its Commission on Chaplains, said of Linzey's long naval career:

"It was my good pleasure and privilege to have served as a military chaplain during part of Stan Linzey's illustrious naval career. I learned to respect and admire Stan especially during our annual military chaplains' conferences/retreats. It was there that a small number of us gathered to discuss the vital moral and ethical issues which we faced regarding our service as chaplains and ministerial relationships with our Fellowship at large.

"Stan impressed me as being a strong spiritual leader with a devout Christian faith that undergirded his entire life and all his family relationships. He has a phenomenal testimony of God's deliverance and help following the sinking of the USS YORKTOWN by the Japanese in World War II. Stan continues to faithfully represent our Assemblies of God Movement as an evangelist.

"Stan and Verna Linzey are the parents of ten children, all of whom are engaged in Christian ministry, chaplaincy, higher education, or Veterans Administration positions. It is particularly noteworthy in the context of this book that three of their sons are military chaplains—George W. Linzey in the Navy, James F. Linzey in the Air Force, and Paul E. Linzey in the Army Reserve. I had the privilege of being present for Jim's swearing in for the Air Force chaplaincy."

Although this book is about one young sailor and his fellow crewmen in the USS YORKTOWN, it is not so much a war story as a personal testimony of the goodness and grace of God. Perhaps anyone could confidently say that God was at Midway, but the man who worked his way up through the torpedoed ship and floated for hours in the surrounding ocean oil slick can declare that fact with authority.

In a time of few war heroes in America, I must admit to a personal objection to the treatment of men and women who have risked their lives on our behalf. After the Battle of Midway, the remaining aircraft carriers all received citations of honor from the President of the United States. It is still a source of pain to the brave survivors who gather annually in memory of the YORKTOWN that the proud ship that now lies on the bottom of the Pacific Ocean received no mention of honor, even though it was a deciding factor in the victory at sea.

Among the many reasons for joining with Stan Linzey on this project, most important is praising God for his protection and guidance, I must emphasize the need in America today to give our military veterans the respect and honor due them.

Throughout this project I have been torn between writing in common English and using the special vocabulary of the Navy. We might use the word boatswain for a warrant officer in charge of the hull and related equipment, but true sailors say bos'n or use such titles as bos'n's mate. Left is port, and right is starboard. Fore is toward the ship's prow, and aft is toward the stern. Floors are decks, and walls are bulkheads. Doors are hatches. Ropes are lines, for the only rope on the ship is the one that rings the bell. And sailors are never on a ship but in a ship; many of them seldom see the light of day. And when they speak of an elevator in an aircraft carrier, or flat top, they do not mean a convenient way for people to get from deck to deck but an apparatus for moving the airplanes between the hanger deck and the flight deck.

Throughout this book we have attempted to maintain the Navy color without becoming incomprehensible to our land-lubber readers.

Stan Linzey himself does not easily surrender his sailor's lingo. Early in his civilian ministry after retiring from the Navy, I had him speak at a church I pastored in Alameda, California. When he gave the altar call, rather than invite the people to come forward to the platform, he summoned them to "the deck."

All Bible references are given in the King James Version, since that would have been the Bible that Stan Linzey would have used in 1942.

People who wish to contact the YORKTOWN (CV-5) Club may write to Chaplain Stanford E. Linzey in care of **Black Forest Press,** 539 Telegraph Canyon Road, Box 521, Chula Vista, CA 91910.

To all the survivors of the USS YORKTOWN (CV-5) and especially to those who so cooperatively shared your stories and photographs, we salute you and thank you for your heroic contribution to the cause of freedom.

David A. Womack
President: Wellsprings Publishers
Springfield, Missouri

PREFACE

It was more than half a century ago that I stood on the deck of the Aircraft Carrier USS YORKTOWN and gazed in awe at the recent destruction of Pearl Harbor. My sailor friends and I were very young then, but a few months later the Battles of the Coral Sea and Midway would make men of us quickly.

Since those decisive days, many fine accounts have been written about those key battles but generally in a secular context for the historian's interest. They have enhanced our knowledge of the war in the Pacific and particularly of those great battles, and we are indebted to them; but there was another side to the story that never has been told.

During that early period of World War II, I was in the U.S. Navy serving as an enlisted musician on the Aircraft Carrier YORKTOWN, which was a major player in the Battles of the Coral Sea and Midway. From my experience in the ship, I observed the supernatural intervention of God played a vital role among both officers and enlisted men. I wish to bring some of that story into focus for the families and friends of the Christian religious community whose loved ones served so heroically in those critical events of the war.

I am writing for all the military personnel who served in those actions and particularly for the survivors of the YORKTOWN and their families and friends. The YORKTOWN (CV-5) Club, which I presently serve as chaplain, meets annually to relive the events and to keep alive the spirit for which we served. I am grateful to the club members for the camaraderie and spirit of fellowship that has endured through the years and are ignited each year anew as we meet together.

I am writing for those many Christians who may not pursue secular history as such but would appreciate reading history that takes into account God's intervening force in the lives and events of the people involved. Many prayed for their men and women during those dark hours of World War II and believed that God heard and answered their prayers; and those of us who benefited from their intercessory prayer continue as witnesses to God's grace.

Divine providence is as relevant today as it was in Bible times. Events do not "just happen." The Battles of the Coral Sea and Midway are cases in point, for we did not win those battles by our wits alone. The odds were stacked against us at Midway; but, in answer to the prayers going on back home in our great nation, the enemy forces made crucial mistakes at Midway. Those errors cost them the loss of ships and men which resulted in their defeat and the turning of the tide in the war.

I am writing to give testimony to God's presence in the most difficult of times and to witness to the saving grace of Jesus Christ. My hope is that this testimony might be an encouragement to others who find themselves in uneven circumstances. Also, I wish to encourage others to be faithful to God and to one another in any and all eventualities, good or bad.

I am writing for my children who have not known what their father went through during the war. One of my daughters wept as she read the account of the sinking of the YORKTOWN and remarked that her brothers and sisters did not know these things.

Finally, I write to remind myself of God's divine favor and providence lest I forget the time when I felt so alone and helpless. Lest I forget. Lest I forget.

I am indebted to many people for the privilege of writing my experiences of the Battles of the Coral Sea and Midway. This book was a formidable task that I could not have done alone.

I began this project at the insistence of David A. Womack, a personal friend and colleague for many years. I had told some of these "sea stories" in the church he pastored in San Jose, California, before he became manager of Ministry Resources Development, in charge of Book Editing and Promotion for Gospel Publishing House in Springfield, Missouri. Everywhere I have spoken, in churches, in colleges, and on military bases, people have expressed great interest. So, when Pastor Womack challenged me to put my story in print, I felt the time had come and agreed to do so.

I greatly appreciate the members of the YORKTOWN (CV-5) Club for their encouragement and willingness to provide information on various people and events that took place in the ship. Gerald B. Fagan, editor of *The Yorktown Crier,* and Peter Montalvo, who preceded him in the publication, have refreshed my memory, on several occasions, with articles in their publication. Bill and Mary Carpenter gave me a picture of the YORKTOWN band marching on the flight deck, taken when they auctioned off the only steak I ever saw on the ship.

William. L. Howard, Pete Newberg, Ralph F. Galluzzo, Morris Bill Frank, Joseph and Margie Kisela, Betty R. Sledge, Fae Marie Smith, and Mrs. Wallace Workman assisted greatly in condensing and abridging the ship's log, thus making it manageable. I greatly appreciate their work, which has enabled me to keep my dates and places straight.

My brother G. Lee Linzey and sister Evelyn Hasbrouck assisted me in remembering events, dates, and places in our early childhood. David Wayne Schreuder, Secretary for General Synod Operations for the Reformed Church in America, from time to time, provided information and counsel.

Mrs. Cecelia "Eva" Kramer of Hacienda Heights, California, the daughter of Mrs. Esther Sandahl, told me again the story of her mother praying in the Spirit for her brother, Photographer Henry "Hank" Johnson, when he was ordered to abandon ship from the USS LEXINGTON during the Battle of the Coral Sea. At the time of this writing, that praying mother is an elderly lady about 88 years of age. She resides in a rest home in Garden Grove, California. The Navy gave no medals for prayer in World War II, but if they had Esther Sandahl would have been a highly decorated hero. She and her husband had been missionaries for many years in China and Malaysia. Hank Johnson now lives in Huntington Beach, California. He has provided some of the action shots of the Battle of the Coral Sea and the LEXINGTON. From time to time, I have had the privilege of speaking with him and reliving the events we once shared.

I have had access to the ship's log, the commanding officer's Report of Action for June 4 and 6, 1942, and his final messages to the Secretary of the Navy and to the Commander of Task Force 17, Rear Admiral Frank Jack "Blackjack" Fletcher, reporting the sinking of the YORKTOWN. This has been of inestimable assistance in writing the story.

Finally, I express my appreciation for Verna May, my dear wife of over fifty-five years, who has supported me in all my endeavors. She has proofread the manuscript, corrected me on some dates and facts, and once again been a patient "Navy Widow" while I wrote.

Having received all this help, I hope the reader will find as much pleasure with *God Was at Midway* as I have enjoyed while writing it.

Through the years in our annual reunions, my shipmates and I have told and relived the stories of the YORKTOWN. We won't let her sink. She may be gone, but she is not forgotten.

Captain Stanford E. Linzey, Jr.,
Chaplain, USN, (Ret.)

Chapter ONE

Dead in
the Water

I was a young sailor on June 4, 1942, when the USS YORKTOWN was sunk in the Battle of Midway. We were only three miles from land—**straight down!** And that is where our great aircraft carrier still rests today as a tomb for some four hundred of our friends whose lives so suddenly ended on that tragic day.

The remaining survivors of our ship's sinking still come together every year at the YORKTOWN (CV-5) Club to exchange war stories. We remember the buddies we left behind when we struggled up through the flooding wreckage of the dying vessel and went over the side into the thick oil slick that covered the rolling Pacific Ocean.

The best of the American and Japanese navies were in full conflict at the Battle of Midway, and we already had taken three bomb hits. Our hanger deck was in flames from one bomb, another had set fire to our fourth deck, and a third had exploded in the stack and blown out the fires in our boilers. We all felt the ominous silence of dead engines as we floated lifeless in the water!

Abandon Ship!

At 2:00 p.m. our engineers had just gotten the ship's engines started again when the next wave of Japanese attack planes came roaring in and dropped their torpedoes for the kill. That was more than a half century ago, and yet I can hear the agitated voice that spoke over the headphones and loudspeakers as if it were yesterday: "Stand by for torpedo attack!"

I can still close my eyes and shudder at the memory of the thudding of the two torpedoes as they struck us on the port (left) side. I was down on the third deck at water level when they blasted the side of our ship and ripped huge holes in our hull, and I can still remember how the ship lifted into the air with the impact of the explosions. As the water rushed in, the great aircraft carrier listed to the port side at twenty-seven degrees until the very edge of the hanger deck was dipping into the water. Inside the ship, there was nothing like a deck or a bulkhead, for every surface was lying at an angle and making it almost impossible to maneuver from one compartment to another. Water mains were broken and spewing forth water, and the lights were out. Only the blue battle lamps illumnitated the scene.

I will never forget the last command of Captain Elliott Buckmaster. A chill went through all of us as we heard his fateful words: "Abandon ship!"

In the following hectic hours, we struggled for survival. We had little time to think of the many friends we were leaving behind in the depths of the ship. If we were having trouble with a loss of electricity and broken water lines at the third deck, surely the men below us were flooded with little hope of survival. Yet, in spite of the jeopardy of our condition, I recall the disciplined calm among our sailors as we worked our way up through the destruction. Well trained for such a calamity, we helped each other find our way to the surface and then slid down two-inch lines into the oil-covered sea.

History has recorded the battle strategies, the mistakes, the glories, and the tragedies of the war at sea. The Battle of the Coral Sea, in which the YORKTOWN was first damaged, turned back the southern expansion of the Japanese Empire; and the Battle of Midway, where she was sunk, was the turning point of the Pacific War. We look back now and see the entire Pacific Theater of the war from beginning to end—the Japanese expansion in Asia and the Pacific Islands, the attack on Pearl Harbor that brought America into the war, the prisoner of war camps, the raising of the U.S. flag on Iwo Jima, the atomic bomb attacks on Hiroshima and Nagasaki, and the signing of the unconditional surrender on the deck of the Battleship USS MISSOURI. Much has been said, written, and documented on film; but what history does not remember is that wars are not composed of the grand battles alone but of the personal challenges, tragedies, sacrifices, and faith of individuals caught up in the greater conflict.

History does not remember that at the very time when the survivors of the YORKTOWN were fighting for their lives, in the thick oil slick that surrounded the sinking vessel, many individuals and churches in America were praying. My own wife Verna was seized with a deep burden for prayer, and just before the battle I had one of the outstanding spiritual experiences of my life. To all that has been written, I am adding my voice to say, "God was at Midway!"

Over the Side

The motion-picture epic *Midway*, starring Charlton Heston, was based on solid research of the major movements in the Battle of Midway. Yet the writers wove

into the war story the lives and crises of fictional char-
acters to add "real-life" drama to the event. We tend to
think of the Pacific War in terms of the deployment of
ships, airplanes, and weapons; but wars are fought by
people, and every one of the real flesh-and-blood sailors
on the YORKTOWN was an individual whose life was
altered or ended on that day. With our tragedy, the lives of
mothers, fathers, wives, and children were deeply
affected. The instant when those torpedoes struck our port
side was but a moment in the whole of the lives of all personnel on board. Every sailor had a story to tell, a family
back home, and a life to live—and four hundred men
gave their lives that day as the price of human freedom.
In the telling of my own story, I wish to somehow represent the many stories of the other men who died or
survived the sinking of the YORKTOWN.

They say your whole life passes before you when you
think you're going to die, but to be several decks down in
a listing ship that may capsize and sink to the bottom of
the sea at any moment, is such an unreal experience that
rather than look at the broader picture of life, we focused
almost totally on the immediate—the wet sloping decks
or the next steel rung of a ladder. I don't ever remember
being afraid as I made my way up and up through the
ship; it was later, while fighting for my life in the thick
ooze of the tossing oil slick, that my life came into focus
as clearly as any motion picture. The Rio Grande Valley
in Texas was my home, not that slimy, choking oil next to
a sinking ship in the middle of the Pacific Ocean.

It was then, in the rolling water, with the hulk of the
listing ship rising above me and hearing men calling to
one another, that my mind went back to Texas almost as if
I were composing my own obituary. Looking back now
and remembering the circumstances, it was incredible that
the oil had not caught fire. All of us would have burned
to death. It also was amazing that no sharks were in the

area, for they had been frightened away by the torpedo explosions.

My Early Life in Texas

I was born in Houston, Texas, on October 13, 1920; but my family soon moved to Kingsville, where my brother Garnet Lee and sister Evelyn were born. We later moved to San Benito in the Lower Rio Grande Valley. I started school in San Benito; but a year later we moved to Harlingen, where I went through the rest of the elementary grades.

With today's advances in refrigeration, it may be hard for some to realize what a large industry the production and delivery of ice once was. At Harlingen, my father was an engineer for the ice plant, which was owned and operated by the Central Power and Light Company. One of the largest ice plants in the nation, it made 400 tons of ice each day and supplied ice for the railroad cars that hauled produce from the Rio Grande Valley, the "garden spot" of the nation. Because of its main business, it was located in the railroad yards; and our family lived in nearby company housing.

Against all rules of safety, the engineers' children were allowed to play in and around the plant and the railroad yards. We crawled in and out and under the trains, not realizing the dangers involved. Adults repeatedly warned us against those activities; but we had fun, and by God's mercy we managed to live to adulthood.

One day we crawled out from under a 35-car train, and just as we emerged from beneath it, to the other side, a switch engine hooked onto it. With a jerk the cars began to roll. A split-second later and we could have been mangled or crushed. That was a close call!

We never told Mother about those escapades.

Ours was a happy life. Though father had an alcohol problem, he never abused us nor caused us suffering. For as long as I could remember, Dad always worked the night shift and slept all day. It was Mother who saw to it that we went to school and church regularly.

We had many pets; a zoo was more like it! Dad always had a pack of 'coon dogs', he and Mother spent many nights down on the Rio Grande River hunting raccoons. The dogs smelled out the raccoons and gave chase; when they treed them and held them at bay, Dad would shoot the raccoons out of the trees. One night they caught a baby raccoon and brought him home. What a guy! We named him Coon. He was playful and mischievous, played with the cat, and became friends with the dogs. They wouldn't hurt him. One morning we woke up to find Coon sitting in the skillet on the kitchen stove eating the grease. He would not turn loose of the skillet nor get out of it.

When Grandmother Royalty visited us from Kentucky, the little raccoon got into her face powder. He sat on her dresser and shoveled out the powder all over the dresser. What a pest!

He liked to get into the bath tub with my brother and me. We gave him ice to play with and watched him try to pick it up. He'd try to fish it out of the water with his little paws, but it was too elusive for him. Raccoons wash everything they eat, so when we gave him cookies he would put them into the water only to see them fall apart in his paws.

Mother had a parrot that Dad gave her before they were married. He had brought the baby bird on his arm across the border from Mexico. Polly was a talker, and he learned to sing duets with Mother. He sang the melody while mother sang alto. He answered the door when someone knocked by saying, "Come in." When we boys played baseball in the front yard, the parrot would watch us while sitting in the big hackberry tree and yell, "You're Out!" He would get us into arguments with each other until we realized it was Polly making the calls. This bird witnessed our births and growth into adulthood, and that of the grandchildren. Polly knew us all.

When I was sixteen, I worked one summer for the WPA (Works Progress Administration) for $1.50 per day—the total sum of $9.00 a week. This was President Franklin D. Roosevelt's job program to put men to work. It was hard work. I helped build the concrete irrigation ditches in South Texas. This was during the Depression and I was glad to have a job and be able to work.

Mother used to go swimming with us in the irrigation canals. They were great swimming holes! One day Mother stepped into a hole in the soft mud on the bottom of a canal that had not yet been concreted and twisted her ankle. I had to carry her out of the canal, and she maintained a limp in her walk until her death many years later.

Before my senior graduation at McAllen High School, the family moved to Mercedes. To allow me to finish with my class, Mother gave her piano to Mr. and Mrs. Hendricks to pay for my room and board with them for the remainder of the school term. It was an amicable arrangement because their son and I played football together on the high school team.

During my school years, I had been involved in numerous activities, including the Boy Scouts. At sixteen, I attained the rank of Eagle Scout and Junior Assistant Scout Master of Troop 13, sponsored by the Lion's Club. I lettered in varsity football on the high school squad, playing guard and tackle while playing right guard during a game I injured my neck and finger in a head-on collision with the left guard...one of us got confused on the play. When we pulled out to run interference for the quarterback, one of us ran in the wrong direction and we crashed head-on into each other behind the center. Sometimes, I still feel the pain in my neck.

I also was the first clarinetist in the high school band. I took many honors in solo competition on the clarinet and in 1936 won the Texas State championship with my mother as my accompanist. We were a great team!

Texas A&M and other schools invited me to apply for music scholarships. Earlier, as a boy nine years of age in Harlingen, I had heard the U.S. Marine Band on tour under the direction of the celebrated bandmaster John Philip Sousa. This was Sousa's last tour, he died shortly after that. Sousa had awarded the Harlingen High School band the First Place trophy in band competition among the bands of the Rio Grande Valley. Back then I decided I would be a Navy musician.

The Navy offered a free music education to high school musicians who could qualify musically and physically. The applicant had to agree to enlist for six years. After graduation from high school, I made application to attend the U.S. Navy School of Music in Washington, D.C.

Graduation from McAllen High School was uneventful for me because I graduated at mid-term and was unable to participate in the parties and proms that went with the festivities.

At Mercedes, Mother had made friends with Mrs. West, the mother of Milton West, our congressman who gave me a recommendation to the U.S. Navy School of Music. As I waited for the application to make its way through channels, I was living with the family in Mercedes. Garnet and Evelyn, both younger than I, were still at home and in school.

Dad had been laid off from the ice plant work, so my parents operated a "Mom and Pop" gasoline station and grocery store in Mercedes; we all lived in one room in the rear of the store. The shower was in an outside enclosure with no roof. The store was part of an old motel complex, run by Mr. Jordan. In 1939, the Great Depression still lingered and no one had any money. Mom was the business manager and salesperson for the store, so she would barter goods with customers to make it work. That was the custom then. One day, a man came into the store and traded Mother a 12-gauge shotgun for a ham. She then traded the shotgun for more groceries. This is how we lived, day to day, from hand to mouth. We did not know we were poor, because no one had told us. Everyone was in the same boat.

In the back room—our only room—we lived and slept on army cots placed side by side so all of us would have a place to sleep. Whoever slept in the middle had to "ride the rails." It was most uncomfortable and back-breaking, but we made it.

As I rode the rails, I could hear the jukebox in the honky tonk restaurant across the street belt out "The Yellow Rose of Texas" or "San Antone Rose." I can still hear them, for such things stay with you. They remind us of our roots, our place and station in life.

Hitchhike to Kentucky

In the Great Depression we had no money, so my brother Garnet and I decided to ride freight trains and hitch-hike our way to Kentucky to visit our grandmother—a trip of about 1,500 miles. In those Depression years, it was a common sight to see men riding freight trains.

At the beginning of our trek, Garnet and I decided to separate and go it alone so we could hitch rides more easily. We planned to meet again in Beaumont, some 300 miles from home; but after we separated we never found each other. In fact, I never saw my brother again for several years due to my Navy life and travels.

Alone and on my own for the first time, I rode trains and thumbed rides to Louisville, Kentucky. It took me three weeks. I met many interesting people on the roads—some good, some not so good—but all interesting. Once I got stranded in Water Valley, Mississippi. To get something to eat, another man and I agreed to unload a railroad car of watermelons. The pay: all the watermelon we could eat. I haven't cared much for watermelon since!

At last, I arrived in Louisville and made my way to Grandmother Royalty's home in Jeffersontown, a suburban town about fifteen miles from Louisville. She welcomed me with open arms. I was so glad to get off the streets and trains and take a bath! I provided company for her for several months.

Due to my relocation from Texas, my application to the Navy School of Music had been transferred to the Kentucky region. Finally, I got word to report to the Navy Recruiting Office in Louisville for my physical examinations for entrance into the U.S. Navy.

During those Depression years, the Navy was very particular in their recruiting program. I had to take four physical examinations. First, I failed because of my teeth. I had to have all necessary dental work done, at my expense, prior to my next examination. Granny came to my aid. On my second exam, I had a temperature of 99.6 degrees, one degree over normal. I failed. They were so picky, I thought. On the day of the third exam, I looked in the mirror while shaving and noticed that my eyes were yellow. "Granny, look! My eyes are yellow!" I hollered. "What'll I do?" This was cause for panic.

She took me to her family doctor who pronounced, "You have yellow jaundice!" We called the Navy recruiting officer and postponed my appointment until further notice. The doctor gave me some large orange pills to take, and I had to stay home until I got well.

On the fourth try, I passed my physical examinations with flying colors and was ordered to the Navy School of Music to take my musical exams on my clarinet. If I could pass these exams, I would be admitted into the school.

The Navy School of Music

I took my orders and my clarinet and caught the train to Washington, D.C., where I took the tests on the clarinet for my examiner, Chief Musician John Liegl, a clarinetist in the U.S. Navy Band. He passed me. So on January 11, 1939, I was sworn into the U.S. Navy with the rate of Apprentice Seaman. I was to attend the Navy School of Music at the Washington Navy Yards in Washington, D.C. My navy career had begun!

In those hours of floating in the heavy oil slick that surrounded our terribly listing aircraft carrier, I remembered the details of my youth with much greater clarity than I can now recall how I survived that awful ordeal. I did not know if I would die in the oil-covered sea, but if I did, I knew I had already lived a good life.

Chapter TWO

The Gathering Storm

Anyone who has seen pictures of sea birds, seals, or other aquatic animals caught in the horrible goo of an ocean oil spill, will have some idea of our pitiful plight as we floated for hours in the churning Pacific Ocean. It was not just oily water but fuel oil mingled with salt water. It produced a gluey ooze several inches thick. We were thoroughly coated with the brown, suffocating substance that continued to gush out from the damaged ship.

History may have remembered us as war heroes, but on June 4, 1942, I did not feel very brave, certainly not heroic. As a frightened 21-year-old sailor tossed about by a threatening sea, I thought I was going to die. With the rest of the fleet caught up in the Battle of Midway, surely the sharks would come before any rescuers could reach us.

Yes, I was a Christian. Mother had made certain her children grew up in Sunday school and church and knew how to call on God for any personal need. Yet, as I struggled just to keep my face above water and the oil out of my eyes, nose, and mouth, the very essentials of survival over–shadowed any further fear of impending death. I thought of my early life and my short navy career, but most of all I longed for my dear young wife, Verna May. I prayed for a miracle, not knowing that during those very hours my wife had felt a great burden of prayer for me. While I struggled for my very life in the Pacific Ocean, Verna May was on her knees in San Diego. Little had I known, as a young sailor in love, what a blessing God had given me. Verna May would pray for me and accompany me in ministry all through the years.

Looking back over my young life, I was grateful to God for my background...and for having trusted in Him for my rescue.

I Begin My Navy Career

I had joined the Navy to play my clarinet with no idea that my instrument would someday lie on the bottom of the Pacific Ocean.

We who passed our entrance tests in Washington, D.C., were sent by steamboat down the Potomac River to boot camp in Norfolk, Virginia, for three weeks of navy orientation. It was January—so cold. We had to scrub our hammocks (the Navy was still sleeping in hammocks at that time) and wash our clothes outside, by hand, in the snow, at five o'clock in the morning. It was a tough new life.

Upon completion of boot camp we sailed on an overnight steamship back up the Potomac River to Washington to begin our music training. The course consisted of music harmony and theory, composition, and endless hours of practice on our instruments. Not only that, but we had to learn to play three instruments. In my case, it was the clarinet for the military band, saxophone for the dance band, and viola for the concert orchestra.

My examiner, Chief Musician John Liegl, later became my instructor on clarinet in the music school. He took a personal interest in me, and a friendship developed. He had previously played first chair clarinet with John Philip Sousa's U.S. Marine Band and had been the examiner for clarinetists who came into Sousa's band. Later, Liegl told me, "Stan, if Sousa were alive today, I'd recommend you for his band." What a great compliment it was for a lad of eighteen!

I practiced and studied hard, finishing my course in an accelerated manner. Then, to add to my honors, I was given an assignment to the Navy's newest aircraft carrier, the USS YORKTOWN (CV-5). In July, 1939, I relieved the ship's band's first clarinetist, who was promoted to the U.S. Navy Band in Washington, D.C. It seemed a good move for both of us.

The YORKTOWN was a state-of-the-art aircraft carrier at that time. New and large, she was the first of her class built as an aircraft carrier from the keel up. Other carriers had been converted from other types of vessels and converted into carriers. Navy ships have hull numbers that designate their purpose. That of the YORKTOWN was CV-5, with "C" designating the ship as a carrier, "V" that it carried aircraft, and "5" that it was the fifth carrier in the U.S. Navy. She was launched on April 4, 1936, and commissioned on September 30, 1937.

The YORKTOWN (CV-5) was the third ship in the Navy to be named YORKTOWN after the city of Yorktown (Town of York), Virginia, where the Revolutionary War battle of 1781 was fought. The first Cruiser YORKTOWN was a sloop-of-war commissioned in 1840. During a deployment, she hit an uncharted reef off the Cape Verde Islands and sank on September 6, 1850.

The second YORKTOWN was a steel-hulled gunboat delivered to the Navy in 1889. This ship was decommissioned and sold in September, 1921.

The aircraft carrier YORKTOWN, CV-5, was

launched on April 4, 1936, and sponsored by First Lady Eleanor Roosevelt. She broke the bottle of champagne across the bow of the ship and exclaimed, "I christen thee, YORKTOWN!" It was commissioned on September 30, 1937. This was our ship.

In its brief service, the great aircraft carrier saw extensive duty both in the Atlantic and the Pacific Oceans. From her commissioning, until the day she was torpedoed and sank on June 7, 1942, she served only four years, eight months, and six days.

Since the sinking of the CV-5, two more ships have carried the name YORKTOWN—an aircraft carrier (CV-10) and a guided missile cruiser (CG-48).

Peter Montalvo, past president of the YORKTOWN (CV-5) Club, got to visit the site of the building of that ship. He saw a video presentation of the laying of the keel of the missile cruiser. President Ronald Reagan had been present for the event, and Secretary of the Navy John Lehman, Jr., mentioned how the YORKTOWN (CG-48) would follow in the wake of the YORKTOWN (CV-5).

Montalvo said, "Shipmates, that's when the tears came. We are not forgotten, it's just that not enough is being told, voiced, or whatever to the American public about the gallantry of the YORKTOWN (CV-5) and the 'true grit and tremendous courage' of its crew in the first six months of World War II." (*Yorktown Crier,* January 1983, page 1)

The YORKTOWN (CV-5) was a 20,000-ton vessel. The flight deck was 825 feet long; the beam was 82 feet, 3 inches; and its draft was 27 feet. That is, it displaced 27 feet of water. Assigned to the ship were 180 officers and 2,135 crewmen, although considerably more than that were on board at the Battle of Midway. She was easily identifiable by the big "Y" painted on the stack and the letters "Y K T N" painted on both ends of the flight deck.

An Eventful Trip

I left the Washington Navy Yards in July, 1939, with orders in my hands sending me to the USS YORKTOWN (CV-5), home ported in San Diego, California. At the Anacostia, D.C., Naval Air Station, I caught a navy hop (military flight), which flew to Barksdale Field in Louisiana. I hitch-hiked from there to my home in Mercedes, Texas, in the Rio Grande Valley. After a brief visit with my parents, I again hitch-hiked to Brooks Field in San Antonio to catch a military flight to San Diego.

On my way to San Antonio, a man who gave me a ride asked where I was going. I replied, "San Diego."

"That's where I'm going," he said.

I thought I was lucky to get a ride all the way to the West Coast, but after a few miles he stopped at a small gas station and country store and said,"Well, we're here!" Indeed we were—San Diego, Texas!

I caught another ride to San Antonio. The navy torpedo plane on which I flew out of San Antonio was an old, out dated biplane that had outlived its usefulness and was being flown to San Diego for "surveying"—that is, to be destroyed. The plane was in bad shape, but it was a free ride. We all had to don parachutes!

There were five of us on the aircraft, so we were crowded. I had to lie on the deck of the plane in my Navy dress blue uniform with a 300-gallon tank of high octane aviation fuel right in front of me. Dangerous! I had to lie on the deck for the whole trip and could not see outside.

We touched down to refuel in Yuma, Arizona, where it was 113 degrees in the shade. We took off, and when we reached an altitude of about 1,500 feet the engine began coughing and spitting, and then failed in mid-air. All of us tensed! Lt. Ottinger put the plane down safely, and the crew had to work on the engine all night. The next morning we took off, crossed over the southern end of the

Rockies, and landed at North Island Naval Air Station in San Diego.

There she lay. The YORKTOWN was tied to the pier. My eyes must have bulged out at the sight, for I had never seen a ship the size of this carrier—not even in Texas! It was so massive I wondered how it could stay afloat. I didn't know the Navy built ships this large.

I reported aboard and was logged in as a member of the ship's company. A messenger took me to the band's quarters on the third deck. This would be my home for the next three years until the ship sank at Midway. I was proud to be assigned to such a wonderful new ship.

On Board the YORKTOWN

When I reported aboard for duty, I was eighteen years old and beginning a seafaring career that eventually would span 28 years and a series of wars. I came on board the YORKTOWN as a seaman second class; many years later I would be a captain and the Command Chaplain in the USS CORAL SEA—an aircraft carrier named for a battle in which I personally participated.

We were awakened by the bugler every morning at exactly six a.m. There were still four bugle-masters in the Navy on active duty. The boatswain piped Reveille over the loud speaker system for all hands. Then his raspy voice would ring out, "Reveille! Reveille! All hands, Reveille! Heave out and trice up! Sweepers start your brooms! Clean sweep down fore and aft! Reveille! Reveille! All hands, Reveille!"

One day the bos'n's mate of the watch dared a young Marine bugler to swing Reveille on his bugle. The Marine took the challenge, and the commanding officer threw him in the brig for three days!

After a shower and shave we had breakfast on the mess decks. On Wednesday and Saturday mornings we had beans and cornbread for breakfast. Oh, yes! I must not forget the prunes. It was not bad when you got used to it, but for a newcomer it was different.

At 7:45 a.m., the ship's band mustered on the flight deck in fair weather, or on the hangar deck if the weather was foul, to play the national anthem for the flag-raising ceremony. This occurs daily on all U.S. Navy ships and stations throughout the world. The band then would practice in the morning hours.

Lunch was at 11:30 a.m., followed by more band practice. Often the band played a concert on the hangar deck for the crew, during the lunch hour, or prior to movies in the evening.

There were more than 2,000 of us in the ship's crew, besides the officers. While the band's duties were to practice and play concerts, the rest of the crew had to swab decks, shine brass work, and paint the ship. I had made a wise choice in becoming a navy clarinetist.

Liberty commenced at 4:00 p.m. each day. We all awaited the bugler's call for liberty, for it meant we could either go ashore or see one of the movies shown on the hanger deck every evening at 7:30, rain or shine.

The carrier had a fine library and reception room, a good place to read, study, or play games. Tennis, badminton, volley ball, and basketball were played on the hangar deck. Were it not for the roll of the ship while at sea, we could have had a bowling alley! But, no way!

"Taps" sounded at ten o'clock each night, generally preceded by the chaplain's evening prayer. The bugler sounded Taps on his bugle. Then the bos'n's mate passed the word, "Taps! Taps! Lights out in all berthing compartments. The smoking lamp is out throughout the ship! Keep silence about the decks. Taps! Taps!" The smoking lamp indicated when the men could smoke

At that time, we operated off the coast of California during the week and went into port in San Diego for the week-ends.

In September, 1939, we went into the Puget Sound Naval Shipyards in Bremerton, Washington, for dry docking: scraping and painting the hull.

While steaming down Puget Sound en route to the shipyards, we traveled at a tremendous speed for a ship our size. Not only that, but it was very foggy in the sound. Every three minutes the captain would ring the ship's bell and blow the whistles. I well remember that it was two whistles with an interval of a twelfth; only a musician would know that.

Suddenly, the ship made a hard turn to starboard (right). Through the mist we saw the ferry Kalakala slip across our bow in the early morning fog. It was on the way from Seattle to the Bremerton Shipyards with many workmen on board going to work. Had we hit the ferry, we would have cut it in half and sunk it immediately with all hands going down. We quickly slowed the great navy vessel.

As the crewmen scraped and painted, the band marched around the drydock playing march music. The band also marched and played for the city of Seattle in an Armistice Day parade. It got tiresome for Seattle is hilly and the streets comport to the hills.

We left the shipyards on December 21, 1939, and steamed south to arrive in San Diego on the 24th, the day before Christmas, to resume a routine schedule.

Verna May

Back in San Diego, the bandmaster, Chief Musician Joe Bush, asked Austin Groves, the baritone player in the YORKTOWN band, to come to his house to meet a young civilian neighbor who also played the baritone horn. The chief had heard the young man play and felt he needed some lessons, perhaps, the bandsman would be willing to tutor him.

Musician Groves and I were close friends, so one day we went into the city together. He was going to the bandmaster's home and I went to a private instructor to take advanced clarinet lessons. As we parted company, I casually said to the bandsman, "Find out if this lad has a sister who plays the clarinet,and I'll come out and give her some lessons." I had other things than clarinets in mind, but little did I know what I was saying in fact would materialize.

Later that night, when we both returned to the ship, the musician said to me, "Hey, Linzey, Delbert's sister plays the clarinet, but her clarinet is broken. You ought to go out and fix it. Her name is Verna—Verna May Hall."

"Aw, come on," I retorted. I didn't believe him, but I accepted his challenge and went with him on Sunday afternoon to meet the young lady. It was true. Delbert did have a sister, and she did play the clarinet. I fixed her clarinet by adjusting a couple of screws. It was very simple, really, but to her I was a hero. We spent the day together playing Monopoly. Then as evening approached, she said to me, "We have to go to church."

Wanting to be with her, I readily assented. Her sister, Burnena Van Horn, an evangelist, was holding a revival meeting in the Assemblies of God Church in National City, California, so we went to hear her. At the conclusion of her message, she invited those to come forward who wished to accept Jesus Christ as their Savior. This had a profound effect on me, for I had a flashback. I was reminded by the Holy Spirit of my experience of conversion, at age nine, in the First Baptist Church in Harlingen, Texas.

Our family had attended the Baptist church, and one Sunday morning Brother Lee, the pastor, had given an invitation to accept Christ. My Sunday school teacher, Miss Prentiss, had asked me if I wished to accept the Lord.When I replied that I did, she accompanied me to the altar and led me in prayer. I will never forget the prayer that the Lord would hold me to. Imagine a nine year-old boy telling the Lord what to do, or not to do. But, I did it. I prayed,"God, forgive my sins and save my soul." But way down deep in the depths of this kid's heart I heard myself mumble, "Just don't make me a preacher."

It seemed even then, I had a precognition of what would later transpire; for me to eventually become a minister. When I went to the altar again that night in National City, I made two decisions: I reaffirmed my faith, coming back into fellowship with Christ, and I accepted the call to preach

Verna May was a Kansas girl. She was a petite five foot three inches in height and weighed about 98 pounds. When my father first met her, he said, "You're no bigger than a bar of soap!" With long brown hair and gray-green eyes, she was vivacious and personable, she had come to San Diego about the same time as I had been assigned to the YORKTOWN.

Her brother Franklin had teased her, "Verna, you'll go to California and marry a sailor." She vehemently assured him she would not. "No, not me," she had said.

Verna's mother, Alice May Doyle, owned some rental properties in San Diego as well as the Crystal Pier in Pacific Beach. I often volunteered to work on the properties and paint them. Anything to be near Verna May. It didn't seem like work when she was there.

At first, I feared she was too young to date. Was I robbing the cradle? Then I found out she was a few months older than I. So, we got along well. Verna lived in South San Diego, so, every day I had liberty, I rode the bus from the ship to her home and back. If I missed the last bus back to the ship, I would take a taxi or would occasionally walk.

Verna was a religious girl. Her step-father, mother, four brothers, and a sister were ordained ministers. She had been to Bible school.

When the ship sailed, we wrote to each other nearly every day. Often our letters crossed in the mail. When we left for Hawaii and returned to Puget Sound, we wrote daily. When mail call sounded, I usually got several letters at once. At first, she signed her letters "Sealed with a kiss," but then it was shortened to "S.W.A.K."

While we had not mentioned marriage at this early date, it seemed apparent to both of us, it was to be. We married eighteen months after we met.

Pearl Harbor, Hawaii

On April 1, 1940, the YORKTOWN made its first trip to Hawaii. I shall never forget the sight of the Aloha Tower—landmark of the islands. The islands were truly Hawaiian then, with everything natural, beautiful, and green. The men of the islands still worked hard in the pineapple fields wearing grass skirts.There were few roads, and no concrete jungles as are so prevalent today. We anchored in Lahaina Roads, the body of water lying between Maui, Lanai, and Molokai.

Lahaina, off Maui, was where the whaling ships used to anchor a century ago. The island girls used to swim out to greet the ships, and the whalers would take them on board to party and revel with the seamen.

When the missionaries arrived, they soon put a stop to this behavior by teaching Christian morals to the islanders. The whalers resented this intrusion into their frivolity and, on occasion, fired the ship's cannons into the village, particularly into the chapel, to vent their frustration.

Maui is a beautiful island resort. Lovely Molokai was where Father Damien spent his life establishing his leper colony, he gave his life for the lepers. And Lanai is the beautiful island of pineapples.

In Lahaina, we went ashore only for a few hours because the town was small and could not absorb a large liberty party for very long. In the evening, the sailors gathered on the pier to await the ship's boats to return to the YORKTOWN.

It was a floating pier, and sailors crowded onto it, filling every inch of it. Many were drinking, and some were inebriated. There was no room to move. The men began a bodily motion swaying from side to side, and soon they got rowdy and out of hand. Each time the group swayed to one side, men fell off into the water. When they swayed to the other side, men fell off on that side. I was thankful I was in the middle rather than on the edge. The ship's boats finally came alongside and took us aboard for the trip back to the ship.

Later, we sailed into Pearl Harbor, a natural inlet that makes a ring around Ford Island, where the Naval Air Station is located. The fleet was at anchor or tied to the piers. The battleships were moored, all in a line, at the piers of "Battleship Row."

Pan American Airways had just inaugurated its China Clipper fleet of flying boats. They flew the first air mail to the islands from the mainland. We were glad to see these flying boats land on the water at Pearl City because we knew they carried news from home.

We watched the Matson Company's liners LURLINE and MATSONIA steam in and out of Honolulu from the mainline with tourists going and coming to and from Hawaii.

It was peace–time, and ours was a peace-time navy. The war had not yet begun, so life was unhurried and uncomplicated. We lay on the decks and suntanned when we did not have the money to go ashore. Liberty was great, though the small pay gave us little to spend.

In those days, I was a seaman second class. My pay was thirty-six dollars a month: eighteen dollars on the first of the month, and eighteen dollars on the fifteenth. But it was good. If we went broke before payday, I would hock my watch and a friend of mine, Musician George P. Weiser, would hock his camera. On pay day we would redeem them and start the process over again.

We had sailed out to Pearl Harbor for what we thought would be a period of normal operations, believing we would return to San Diego in two or three months. Instead, we went back to Puget Sound and the shipyards for an overhaul in May. Again, the band played dockside, marching around the dry dock as the crew worked.

At this time, we had a radar antenna installed on the "Mighty Y"—the first of its kind. The crew nicknamed it the "Bed Springs" because it looked to us like a bed springs rotating on the mast. The YORKTOWN was the most well-equipped carrier in the entire fleet.

We returned to San Diego on June 1, 1940, and set sail again on the 7th for Pearl Harbor, to operate in Hawaiian waters for the next three months. We anchored in Lahaina Roads on the 13th.

I had only a few days in San Diego that June, but I had to see Verna May. I bought some Hershey almond chocolate bars in the Navy Exchange to woo her. She gave some of them to her mother, who took a liking to me. This helped our romance! It was still taking the bus or walking to or from the ship.

One Sunday, the chaplain invited Verna and her sister Burnena, the evangelist, to come aboard to attend Divine Service. Burnena played a piano solo, one of her own compositions—"Our Best for Christ." Then we had lunch on the carrier. They thought this was a real treat, and so did I.

At a picnic in Balboa Park one Sunday afternoon (after we both had played in the church orchestra at the Foursquare Church), I learned an important lesson about Verna May. After lunch we had two bottles of Coca Cola, and afterwards (in those days before litter laws) I threw them away in the brush. Verna asked, "Isn't there a deposit on those bottles?"

"Yes," I said. "Three cents."

"Why don't you pick them up and return them?" she asked.

"Okay," I said.

Verna told me later that her thoughts, at the time, were for us to be saving our money if we ever planned to get married. She is frugal, and this lesson has continued through our lives together.

My Christian Ministry Begins

During this time, I had become involved in religious studies and activities. My call to preach at age nine, buttressed by my recent decision to rededicate my life to Christ had begun to have its effect. I knew the Holy Spirit was at work in my life and so I began to spend more and more time reading my Bible. As Jeremiah said, *"But His word was in mine heart as a burning fire shut up in my bones, and I was weary with forebearing, and I could not stay."* **(Jeremiah 20:9)**

While we were in Hawaii this second time, the leader of the Bible class in our sister ship, the USS ENTERPRISE (CV-6), invited me to come over to them and speak one night. On finishing my study with them, I asked them to pray that we could get a Bible study going in the YORKTOWN.

The leader notified me that a study group was being held in the YORKTOWN and they told me who was leading it. I located the leader and found it to be a very exclusive group. In particular, no Pentecostals were-desired. We had some words about it, for I was fast becoming a Pentecostal preacher.

There were two acknowledged Pentecostal believers in the ship—a ship's cook, Rassmussen, and myself. We had good fellowship.

The two of us met the leader of the Bible group to see if we could work together amicably. Finally, in desperation, the leader said, "I am going to pray that God takes you fellows off the ship or takes me off."

God must have answered his prayer, for within two months he received orders to leave the ship. So we were free to start the Bible study. This group was to be all-inclusive, for men of all faiths, it would eventually lead many men to Christ.

The ship's cook was transferred shortly after, which put me in the position of leadership. I had to go it alone. I organized the group, and we began to meet on a weekly basis. This continued until the day the ship sank at Midway.

The plan for the meetings was simple. We met one night each week for fellowship and prayers. We opened with hymns and choruses, followed by prayer requests and testimonies which encouraged others to have faith in God and in His providential care. We then had a brief reading of the Scriptures with appropriate comments. The chaplain got us permission to meet in one of the flight ready-rooms. These are the rooms where pilots congregate to be briefed for flight operations. Men of all faiths were invited.

One day while I was on watch on the forward gundeck, on the starboard side, a messenger approached me and asked, "Are you Linzey?"

"Yes, I am," I replied.

"The executive officer wants to see you," he said.

What could have happened, I wondered, that Commander Jocko Clark wanted to see me? With a sense of foreboding, I went with him to the commander's cabin.

As I was admitted to his room, Commander Clark looked up and asked,"Are You Linzey?" I replied that I was.

"What have you got going on down there?" he probed.

Assuming that I knew what he was getting at, I replied, "Commander, we have an interdenominational Bible class that meets twice a week for men of all faiths and denominations. We meet in the flight ready-room for Bible reading, prayers, testimonies, and hymns. We pray for our families, the nation, and for the officers and crew of our ship."

The veteran naval officer heard it for the first time and was impressed."Has the chaplain been invited?" he asked

"Yes, Sir, he has," I responded. "He gave us permission and the place to hold our meetings."

"Good," he said. "Carry on. I'm glad to hear it. Keep up the good work."

Condition Zebra

One day in September, we went to sea from Pearl Harbor for operations in which experienced seamen would teach us neophytes to sight submarines at sea. It is difficult for the uninitiated to spot a submarine underway.

Submarines are a constant threat to surface ships. They lurk under water to attack ships either early in the morning, or at dusk, when visibility is poor. Lookouts have a hard time spotting them during those hours. The crew sets"Condition Zebra," complete water-tight integrity throughout the ship. All hatches are battened down and secured in case of a submarine attack.

We were on the flight deck watching while the Submarine SHARK came alongside and steamed with us in a parallel formation along our starboard side (the right side of a ship looking forward). After some time, we learned what to look for in spotting submarines. We learned to spot its periscope.

The submarine dived and surfaced again and again. Then it went forward on the starboard side (right) of the carrier, crossed over in front of our bow to the port side (left) and turned and headed back into the direction of the YORKTOWN.

The sub meant to come along our port side. But the helmsman had apparently become confused and lost his orientation as to his location in relation to our ship. So he mistakenly angled into the direction of the carrier. We were on collision course. We watched the maneuver for further developments.

When only moments away, the submarine skipper upped his periscope only to see a huge gray steel wall looming in front of him. Realizing his predicament and his position, he downed his periscope and crash-dived his submarine in an attempt to go under the carrier and thus avoid collision and perhaps loss of life.

On the flight deck, we ran over to the starboard side to see if the submarine would make it under and clear the ship. The submarine would easily be visible since the water around the islands are beautifully blue and clear.

It was a horrendous sight. The SHARK came from under the carrier, but had not dived deep enough to clear the massive keel. When it emerged from under the ship, it immediately surfaced like a giant balloon filled with air. It had scraped our bilge keel (the keel on the side of the bottom to maintain stability of the ship at sea) and had severely damaged its conning tower.

The signalman scrambled to the deck of the submarine and, with his semaphore flags, began signaling for help. The submarine was spouting water some fifty or sixty feet into the air from inside the vessel and had to be towed into Pearl Harbor for repairs. Fortunately, no one was injured.

Chapter
THREE

Romance Blooms into Marriage

We returned to San Diego on October 20, 1940, and operated off the coast of California until November 5–a date to remember for the YORKTOWN, for we would never again operate out of San Diego except for one brief visit.

Back in San Diego again, I pursued my romantic interest with Verna May. Every opportunity I had in those few days I went to her house. Sometimes I stayed too late and missed the last bus into town; then I had to walk or take a taxi to get back to the ship.

Once again, I helped her brother do some painting on the house, anything to be with Verna May.

A Change of Oceans

On November 5, we sailed out of San Diego for what we thought would be a normal period of operations, but we sailed back to Hawaii and operated in and around Pearl Harbor for the next five months.

In March, 1941, I finally asked Verna May to marry me. Her parents had moved to Santa Cruz, California, to pastor a church. On the day when she got my letter, she opened it and was reading as she walked back to the house."Oh," she exclaimed, "he has finally asked me to marry him!" Then she thought, "I wonder why he waited so long?" Then she realized that I had waited because, in those days, a sailor had to be a Petty Officer Second Class or above before the Navy would allow him to marry. I had to be a Musician Second Class. This rule insured that the person had enough money on which to live.

On April 20, 1941, we set sail from Pearl Harbor for more normal operations, but two days later the captain announced he had been given sealed orders to report to the Atlantic Fleet and the Naval Operating Base in Norfolk,Virginia. So we changed course and set our compass for the Panama Canal. I would not see Verna again until the week I married her on July 13, 1941. We had no time to say our good-byes, nor was there time to supply our ship for the trip. We just had to go.

We headed south and took the great ship through the locks of the Panama Canal. We crossed the canal late at night on May 6, so as not to call undue attention to ourselves. Prior to entering the canal, from the Pacific side, we changed the name of the ship to WASP. The ship's welders spot-welded a steel patch with the name WASP over YORKTOWN on the stern of the ship, and painters painted out the big black "Y" on the stack. The Navy Department did not want the Axis powers to know the U.S. Navy was moving one of its aircraft carriers from the Pacific fleet to the Atlantic.

After going through the first locks of the canal near Panama City and crossing the inland lake, we were lowered again to sea level at the locks near Colon and steamed out into the Caribbean Sea. We passed Cuba,

Haiti, and the Dominican Republic then headed north up the east coast of the United States to Virginia. Short of supplies, we ate spaghetti and beans for many of our meals. But we had plenty of coffee, a navy staple.

Coming up past Florida, Georgia, and the Carolinas along the eastern seaboard of the United States, I had an attack of appendicitis and was in the ship's sick bay for much of the cruise. On arrival in Norfolk, I was taken off the ship by stretcher, and confined to the Naval Hospital in Portsmouth,Virginia. The attack proved to be chronic rather than acute, but the doctor advised surgery to preclude any future difficulty I might encounter. So, I went in for a routine operation.

Married to Verna May

I was healing nicely from my surgery when a brilliant idea came to mind. I figured I should be able to get sick leave out of this. Knowing the hospital command did not want to grant extended leave periods, I asked the doctor on the ward, "Doc, will I be able to take leave after I get out of here?"

A Naval Reserve doctor on active duty for the duration of the war, he replied sympathetically, "They won't give anybody leave in this hospital."

"Doc, will you sign my leave request?" I asked.

"Surely. Get it to me," he replied. I filed my request for leave without much faith it would be granted, but it was worth a try. I wanted to get married.

Thinking and feeling that the hospital command would likely cut my request for leave in half, I asked for thirty days sick leave, explaining that I needed time to go to San Diego from Norfolk and return. I remarked I had not seen my parents for a long time, but I said nothing about my plans to meet Verna and get married while on sick leave.

I stood at attention before a medical warrant officer who appeared to me that he thought he owned the hospital or was paying our salaries out of his own pocket. Therefore, he did not wish to grant leave to any sailor. He queried me for ten minutes, quizzing me about the need for thirty days leave. Finally, he said to the yeoman, "Give him fourteen days."

I had won. I had figured correctly, because I wanted fourteen days leave, asked for thirty, and got fourteen. My plans would work out. I could go home.

At the time, Verna was working as a governess to a little girl in Rio Del Mar, a suburb of Aptos, a small town near Santa Cruz, California. I wired her about my appendectomy and then wrote that I had been granted fourteen days sick leave, and that I could meet her on the West Coast so we could get married. We would return to Norfolk and the ship. But she came up with a better idea.

Verna resigned her job and traveled by automobile with a Nazarene minister and his wife who were driving to Mexico City from San Diego. The trip took them down through the Rio Grande Valley of Texas. She shared expenses.

The minister let Verna off in Mission, Texas, and proceeded down into Mexico; Verna caught a bus to McAllen, five miles south, where we had agreed to meet.

So, she told the ticket master that if a sailor came asking for her she would be at the post office a couple of blocks around the corner. When I got to the bus station, he told me where she was and I hurried to the post office where I saw her talking to Mr. Paul, a postal worker and old family friend. She had asked him if he knew Stan Linzey, and Mr. Paul said, "Sure, he went to school with my boys. Hey, there he is now!" I hugged and kissed her, lifting her right off the floor. We had not seen each other in nine months.

In my brother's 1932 Chevrolet sedan, I drove her to my parents in Mercedes. I lodged her in the Mercedes

Hotel, and we were married at 5:00 p.m.. on Sunday, July 13.

We planned a lawn wedding, and Dad engaged the Baptist pastor, Brother Lawson, to officiate. At my parent's home, we had a nice, inexpensive lawn wedding under the big palm tree. My fear, during the ceremony, was if I dropped her wedding band in the heavily matted carpet grass I would never find it. But all went well. Pastor Lawson had to hurry away to get to his church for the Sunday night service.

We spent our wedding night in the Mercedes Hotel, where before consummating our vows we knelt by the side of the bed and prayed, "Our Heavenly Father, we thank you for bringing us together and uniting us as one. We commit ourselves to each other and to You. We pray you bless our marriage. The children that may come from our union we dedicate back to you. Amen."

The following day we took the train to Norfolk, Virginia, where the YORKTOWN was homeported. We did not have the money for a Pullman car, so we took a coach car and had to sit up all the way; we slept intermittently by leaning our heads on each other's shoulders. It was tiring.

The ship was not in port when we returned, so I was ordered to the USS RANGER, another aircraft carrier, until my ship came back into port. In the RANGER, I played in the ship's band for about two months while awaiting the YORKTOWN's return.

Verna and I attended Glad Tidings Assembly of God Church in Norfolk, pastored by Reverend Arthur Graves. The pastor was a fine man of spiritual qualities, a good preacher and counselor. He was a pleasant man, though he neither joked nor laughed much.

We rented a room from Mrs. Detweiler. It was just a bedroom, no kitchen, and little privacy. We just had a screen to shield the doorway. We ate cold sandwiches and cold cereal. We had to share the bath.

Soon after we moved to the home of Mrs. Thornhill, a member of the church. She rented us a small apartment with a bedroom, a kitchenette, and bath. Now we had hot meals. Verna was a good cook. And now we had privacy. We stayed with Mrs. Thornhill until the attack on Pearl Harbor in December.

A Final Thanksgiving of Peace

The YORKTOWN had been ordered to the East Coast to cruise the North Atlantic patrol, escorting ships and materiel from Newfoundland to England. Hitler's U-boats had been wreaking havoc with allied shipping. England was being strangled. By December, 1941, the Nazis had 230 submarines, which had sunk some 366,644 tons of allied shipping with their wolf packs. Later, they were sinking 100,000 tons of shipping per week with a great loss of life.

The YORKTOWN and her escort ships were the first of the U.S. fleet to put into Placentia Bay, Newfoundland, in September, 1941, and Casko Bay, Portland, Maine, just prior to the declaration of war. We sailed into Portland on October 13, my twenty-first birthday. To go ashore we rode on an open motor launch seven miles to shore from the carrier on cold and choppy seas, bouncing a boatload of sailors like a cork on the water.

While in Portland, I had gone ashore and met the Reverend James R.Hicks, pastor of Hephzibah Church, and his wife Mildred. He invited me to his home, a 28-room house, in which he and his family lived and conducted a Bible school. The fellowship was warm and friendly.

One night in November, we were sitting around the table eating doughnuts and sipping coffee when the pastor said, "Call your wife and invite her to come up and stay with us while you are here and spend Thanksgiving with us."

"You mean it?" I asked.

"Surely. Go ahead. Use the phone." So I called.

Verna was working at J.C. Penney's in Norfolk to help us make it financially. When I called she said, "I'm so glad you called. I'm tired of working anyway. I'll come right up." She caught the next train to Portland.

I thought I would surprise my wife with a gift, so I bought her a nice Longine Wittnauer wristwatch. However, in making my purchase I was late in getting to the train. She has not forgotten it to this day.

She had baked an apple pie for me, wrapped it in a newspaper, and brought it along on the train. It was a little soft, the juice was runny, and on the train the pie leaked on her dress. But when she arrived we ate the pie, and it was excellent!

We enjoyed the Hicks family. The pastor was a Gypsy and a man of great humor. He was jovial—always laughing—with a twinkle in his eye. Sister Hicks was a wonderful pastor's wife, a motherly lady, and a good cook. They had three daughters, Priscilla, Gloria, and Evangelyn. They were nearly our age. We also became friends to a couple of the young men in the Bible school, Carl Lindberg and Warren Kelley. Kelley later joined the Navy, and Carl O.Lindberg, Jr., married Gloria Hicks, entered the ministry, and became a leader in the church. He also became the district superintendent of the Northern New England District of the Assemblies of God.

In late November, 1941, right after Thanksgiving, we got orders to return to Norfolk from Newfoundland. Verna went back home by train, and I went back on the ship—a difficult thing to do after being with my young wife and many new friends.

Storm at Sea

We steamed south through some of the worst storms I ever encountered in my navy career. By all accounts, the

North Atlantic is one of the coldest and roughest seas to be found anywhere in the world, especially in the winter. The cold is numbing, and the winds blow hard.

On the way south from Newfoundland, going past Boston Harbor to Norfolk, we ran into a storm that broke "green water" over the flight deck of the YORKTOWN. "Green water" means it is solid water, neither foam nor mist. That meant the waves had to be about 80 feet high to sweep over the flight deck. This was dangerous! All hands were ordered to stay below decks due to foul weather. We could have been washed over the side by the huge waves.

The carrier, large as it was, twisted, turned, and listed from port to starboard as the winds and water burst around the bulwarks. At times, it seemed the ship might not right itself after a hard roll. It trembled and shook as if trying to decide to remain on even keel.

The new recruits on board for their first cruise were lying on the decks like dead men, seasick and nauseous. The rest of us, seaworthy and a bit smug, walked around or over them as we went about our duties.

The carrier burst a seam according to one rumor. The destroyers—"smallboys," as we called them—could not take the weather and had to put into Boston Harbor.

The bows of the battleships astern of us ("battle wagons," as the sailors call them) due to their weight would ride over one wave and sink under the next two. It was a frightening sight.

We rode out the storm and were to undergo an overhaul period in the Portsmouth Naval Shipyards upon our return. Finally, we arrived in Norfolk on December 2, 1941; I rejoined my wife at Mrs. Thornhill's. Little did we know that the storm the YORKTOWN had just come through would be nothing compared to the world wide war storm that would strike just five days later.

Looking back on that storm off the East Coast of the United States, I later wrote the following poem.

THE STORM

For many years I sailed the seas,
    I've seen them great and small;
I've seen the waters rage on high,
    I've seen them rise and fall.

The voyage began and fair winds blew,
    The crew with spirits high;
As the day wore on their tempers waned,
    Ill-omened was the sky.

The clouds grew dark, and the winds blew hard,
    The boat was tempest tossed;
The thunder peeled and the lightning cracked,
    We thought we'd all be lost.

The storm arose as the night grew black,
    The crew in restless fear
Sat huddled in groups upon the deck;
    We thought the end was near.

"Has anyone ever prayed?" cried one,
    In a strained and fearful tone;
It seemed no one could answer back,
    We felt so much alone.

A voice then spoke out from the dark,
    From a man no one could see;
"I do remember a prayer," said he,
    "I learned at mother's knee."

"Then say the prayer," they called aloud,
    "Say it for all on board;
Perhaps He'll hear our prayer tonight,
    Please call upon the Lord."

The voice rang out both loud and clear,
From the depths of the stormy sea;
   "Lord, Remember me," he called,
"O, Christ, Remember me."

The Lord looked down from heaven that night,
   On the men who huddled there;
In answer to the one who prayed,
   The day broke bright and fair.

The waves were calm and the boat set sail,
   On the winds and a sprightly breeze;
The clouds were gone and the sun appeared,
   We sailed with following seas.

When after many days at sea
   The shore loomed into sight;
The spirit of the crew revived,
   'Twas the end of an endless night.

We put the ship into the cove,
   We dropped the hook and moored;
The crew safe in fair havens berthed,
   The journey now was o'er.

Stanford E. Linzey
May, 1992

Chapter Four

Destruction at Pearl Harbor

When we arrived in Norfolk on December 2, 1941, we were expecting a long-awaited overhaul period. Repairs to the YORKTOWN had been postponed a couple of times, and the ship was in need of some work. At this time, we thought we might have six months in port for rest and time with our families, for we had steamed over 17,000 nautical miles in 1941.

Once again, Verna and I were together in our room at Mrs. Thornhill's home. Having attained the rate of Second Class Petty Officer, I was making $72.00 per month. We did not own very much, but Verna and I had each other. We did not know we were poor or deprived, because no one had told us. Like many people, we just made it from month to month, but we were happy.

Verna was frugal, having been raised in a minister's home, so we always scraped by and paid the bills. We took no newspaper and did not even own a radio, so we could not keep up on world events during what turned out to be historic days.

In those few days at Norfolk, church was our life. We attended Glad Tidings Assembly of God with the Reverend Graves as our pastor. Although the world was about to change, we continued on, blissfully unaware of the forces of war that were about to disrupt our lives. The YORKTOWN had justcome through its dangerous assignment in the Atlantic, and we honestly thought we were in for some months of quiet.

Day of Infamy

On Sunday evening, December 7, Verna and I went to church as was our custom when I was in port; and Pastor Graves seemed surprised to see us. His first greeting was, "Did you know that Pearl Harbor was bombed?"

Flippantly, I replied, "You're kidding!" Pearl Harbor must have been the best-defended and least vulnerable port in the world. Then, realizing that the pastor was serious and was neither joking nor laughing, I asked, "When?"

He said, "This morning about eight o'clock Hawaii time. You'd better call the ship and find out if you need to go back."

Totally surprised, I called the officer of the deck, who told me to return to the ship at the regular time on Monday morning at 7:30 a.m., at the expiration of liberty. This meant there would be no overhaul period. War time security was immediately set on board.

Early in the afternoon on Sunday, December 7, the YORKTOWN's radio had picked up a flash message telling of the Japanese attack on Pearl Harbor. Over 2,400 civilian and military personnel had been killed and over 900 wounded. Many ships had been sunk and scores of planes destroyed.

The next day, December 8, President Franklin D. Roosevelt addressed the joint session of Congress and asked that a state of war be declared on Japan. He called the bombing of Pearl Harbor on December 7, 1941, a "Day of Infamy." The President's message was piped over the ship's loud speaker system for all hands to hear.

The President's words were inspiring but horrendous. We had no idea, at that time, what all this would mean to us. We would be living on a day-to-day basis, meeting exigencies as they arose. Later, we would realize it would be a matter of survival. No doubt, we would be steaming back to the vast Pacific Ocean.

On December 13, we went into the dry dock at Portsmouth Naval Shipyard but only to scrape and paint the hull. The extensive over haul had been canceled, and many new shipmates had been ordered aboard for transfer to the Pacific.

On December 16, we moved out of dry dock and moored alongside Pier 7 at the Naval Operating Base in Norfolk. We embarked the air group and supplied the ship. Then suddenly came orders to set sail.

Back to the Pacific

It was pay day, and all the crew had been paid. Now, with the ship reparing to sail, I had to get money to Verna before leaving. But how? Liberty had been cancelled, and no one could go ashore.

There were telephone booths on the pier, and sailors were queued up in long lines behind each booth. Each man was trying to make that last call home to mothers, fathers, and girl friends anywhere and everywhere in the United States. I ran over the side of the ship without obtaining permission from the officer of the deck. I could not find him, so I just ran out and got in line like the others.

The executive officer appeared on the quarter deck and yelled across the pier to us, "You people get back aboard this ship immediately!" I was not about to give up my place in the line after waiting for so long, nor did others obey the order. Finally, I got to a phone.

"Verna," I said, "this is Stan. We got paid today and I have some money for you. Liberty has been cancelled, so I can't come out to the house. Come down to the ship now, and I'll try to get off the ship to give you the money."

It was late in the afternoon, and finally at dusk Verna came traipsing down the pier. Again without permission, I ran over the side and met her and handed her the money.

"Listen," I said. "We don't know whether we're just going out for operations and return or going through the Panama Canal and back up to San Diego. But, do not leave Norfolk until you hear from me. Do you understand?" I had no idea how I would inform her.

She agreed that she did understand, and with that I kissed her and ran back up the gang plank just as the crane on the dock was hoisting it off the pier. Verna returned to the apartment, and at 9:08 p.m. we steamed out of Norfolk.

The "N" Division (navigators) was berthed in the same compartment with the band and the ship's cooks. Many of us became friends, so I asked one of them, "Are we going on operations then return to Norfolk, or are we going around to the West Coast?"

"We don't know, yet," he said, "but we'll know by this time tomorrow night." It turned out that we were heading south to pass through the Panama Canal and up to San Diego. Now I had the problem of getting the word to Verna.

After sailing down the East Coast of the United States and going past Cuba and across the Caribbean Sea, we arrived in Panama on December 21st. The ship's log read:

"21 December 1941: 0400 - 0800 Entered Panama Canal. Gatun locks, second lock, third lock. 1032 Cleared Gatun Lock. 1346 Entering Pedro Miguel Lock. 1434 Miraflores Lake channel. lst lock, 2nd lock, 1635 Cleared 2nd lock, Balboa Harbor, Canal Zone."

This time when we went through the Panama Canal we covered the name YORKTOWN on the stern with the name ENTERPRISE—another attempt to confuse the enemy powers. We passed through the locks, transited the canal, and anchored in Balboa Harbor on the Pacific side in the evening.

There at our Panama Canal military installation I went ashore to send Verna a message by Western Union. Security was strict, and all wires and messages were screened and censored for security purposes. Names of places could not be given out for fear that YORKTOWN's location and destination might be revealed to the enemy. At first, I was puzzled, but after a few moments I figured it out. Verna was from San Diego, so I sent her the message, "Take everything. Go home. Stan." End of problem!

The crew of the YORKTOWN spent our Christmas of 1941 underway from Panama to San Diego. It was not much of a Christmas. When we arrived in San Diego on December 30 and tied up to the pier at North Island Naval Air Station, Verna was there waiting for me.

The YORKTOWN took on provisions at San Diego, and on January 6th we got underway again and headed west to join the fleet in the Pacific. We did not know it at the time, nor could we have known it, but exactly five months to the day, from the date of our sailing—January 6, 1942—the USS YORKTOWN would be sunk by the Japanese in the greatest naval engagement ever fought by superpowers. The YORKTOWN would never return home again.

Into the War

When we sailed out of San Diego, we did not go directly to Hawaii but steamed some 5,000 miles to bomb the Marshall and Gilbert Islands. On the way, YORKTOWN escorted a Marine Brigade to Samoa to bolster its defenses. The Marines were sailing in the Matson Lines ships MATSONIA, LURLINE, and MONTEREY, two of which I had previously seen at Hawaii.

The Marshall Islands, populated by Micronesian people, comprise an area of about 700 square miles. The Japanese had seized the islands in 1914, after which in 1920 the League of Nations had mandated the islands to them. Jaluit and Kwajalein were the major islands. Little did I know then, that someday Assemblies of God missionaries would work to evangelize the Marshalls for Jesus Christ and establish churches in those islands.

The Gilbert Islands comprise about 102 square miles. Tarawa and Makin were the principal islands. Although those islands were a British protectorate in 1892 and became a colony in 1915, they were occupied by the Japanese in 1941 and liberated by the U.S. forces in 1943.

Those of us in the ship experienced little action during that first participation in the war. We saw our aircraft take off from the flight deck, and the pilots returned with reports of accomplished missions. Our task was to preclude the Japanese from assembling their forces there or using their bases in the islands. It was a detracting operation. It diverted the enemy and made him utilize forces that he might have used to better advantage elsewhere in the Pacific.

Our First Damage

Far out in the Pacific, on January 17 the Oiler KASKASKIA came alongside the YORKTOWN to refuel it; but, due to inclement weather and high seas, the ship rammed the YORKTOWN. The log reads:

"17 January 1942: 1445 commenced receiving fuel from KASKASKIA.1644 KASKASKIA came in close alongside again and this time scraped sides, resulting in a broken boom aft on the KASKASKIA, and on the YORKTOWN, some damage to the ship's side and #1 motor launch. 1646 KASKASKIA came in close and scraped again causing additional damage. Tow line parted."

The actual event was a little more colorful than was recorded in the log. Our executive officer, Commander Joseph J. "Jocko" Clark (later Admiral Clark) got angry and jumped up and down on the bridge with his game leg. He screamed at the officer of the deck in the KASKASKIA words to the effect of, "Move your ship, or I'll sink you on the spot!" The oiler had scraped the YORKTOWN, doing damage to the side of the ship and breaking some frames in the pipe shop.

On January 31 our pilots shot down a Japanese Kawanishi flying boat.These huge airplanes were the eyes of the Japanese fleet. They had four engines, a wing span of 132 feet, and a range of 3,000 miles. Our pilots spotted it as it came out of the clouds about noon. They fired on it, and it exploded and fell apart, scattering debris over the ocean. There was much cheering on the decks of the YORKTOWN.

The ship's log reads: "1313 sighted enemy [Japanese] bomber, 4 engine type, high wing monoplane, bearing 060 (T), distance 10 miles, target angle 000. 1314 changed course to port to bring guns to bear on enemy plane. 1315 enemy plane crossed bow of ship to port and passed behind cloud, pursued by two planes of the combat air patrol. 1317 enemy plane bearing 335 (T), distance 5 miles, was shot down in flames by two pilots of the combat air patrol."

TO RA, TO RA, TO RA

On February 6, just two months after the infamous Japanese attack, we sailed into Pearl Harbor for the first time since the beginning of the war. Hundreds of sailors manned the rails on the flight deck. This was a fair weather parade, an old navy custom for ships going into port. It is a form of greeting. All hands were in white uniforms.

As we approached the Island of Oahu, with the famous Diamond Head far off to our right, and the island's Leeward Side off to our left, we eased the great aircraft carrier into the ship channel of Pearl Harbor. People lined the beach along the channel and cheered us. We felt good about it. It was nice to be liked and appreciated. We were a proud bunch. We had just concluded a successful-bombing mission on the Marshall and Gilbert Islands and our fame had preceded us.

The USS YORKTOWN was the flagship of Task Force 17 (TF-17), as ENTERPRISE was the flagship of TF-8. An aircraft carrier does not sail alone but always in the company of other ships for protection—usually with a cruiser and several destroyers, which we affectionately called "tin cans".

As we rounded the bend of the ship channel and approached Ford Island, we got the surprise and shock of our lives—a sight we could not believe and would never forget. For the first time, we looked on the incredible destruction of Pearl Harbor.

The sailors, normally a happy and jovial group on entering port, could only stare in stunned silence as they viewed the scene. This was not the way we remembered Pearl Harbor nor the great American fleet. No one felt like talking; there was nothing to say. Emotions were stirred. All of the crew stood rigidly silent as we viewed the devastation.

Commander Mitsuo Fuchida had launched and led,

from the Japanese aircraft carriers, his attacking squadrons against the island bases with his now famous, "TO RA, TO RA, TO RA."

Some have interpreted this signal as a code expression to read, "TIGER, TIGER, TIGER." However, Thomas B. Allen (*National Geographic*,December 1991, page 5) points out that this signal comprised two words—"To" and "Ra". "To" was the signal to attack, and "Ra" was the signal given to announce that the raid had been a complete surprise.

Truly, it was a surprise, and for those of us who stood on the deck of the YORKTOWN that day it was an unbelievable sight. How could we reconcile the destruction that lay before us with the impression of invincibility the Navy had so well instilled in us? The war had been a kind of game to us until then, but that day, as we entered Pearl Harbor, the game ended and we were thrust into a life-and-death struggle to avenge America and defeat Japan.

Battleship Row was in total disarray, for eight U.S. Navy battleships had been bombed, torpedoed, and sunk at their piers. Oil, many inches thick, covered the water from the leaking hulls of the ships that had been torpedoed, and they were still leaking. Trash and debris covered the surface of the water. No spit and polish here. No time to clean up the mess, yet. The pride of the Battle Group Command was a graveyard.

The Battleship USS NEVADA had made a run for the open sea to escape the impending disaster; but it was bombed and torpedoed and ran the risk of sinking and blocking the harbor. The commanding officer beached his ship astern to save it and keep the harbor open.

The Battleship USS OKLAHOMA was torpedoed and capsized. It lay on its side in forty feet of water, the average depth of the port. In that ship alone, 415 men died; and one of our navy bands went down.

The target ship, the Battleship USS UTAH had capsized, turning bottoms up, hull in the air, and mast in the mud. Some 112 men died in that ship, and 58 remain entombed. A target ship is used in bombing, torpedo, and gunnery practice by our own forces. The purpose is not to hit it but to practice on it. Quite often it tows a sleeve as a target for ships or planes to fire upon. Aircraft make practice bombing and diving attacks on the target ship. The UTAH was no longer battle ready and therefore was used as a target ship.

The Battleship USS ARIZONA, the flagship for the Battle Group Commander, received several bomb hits. One 1,760-pound bomb, an armor-piercing shell, hit the forward magazine, which exploded and blew up the ship. It blew 120 feet off the bow, according to one account. On the ARIZONA, 1,177 men died. Her mast melted in the heat and fell to a forty-five-degree angle amidst a billow of smoke that rose a thousand feet into the air.

The commanding officer, Captain Van Valkenburgh, and the Battle Group commander, Rear Admiral Isaac C. Kidd, were blown to bits on the bridge. Many men, trying to escape the fires and shrapnel, leaped screaming into fiery, oily water only to perish in so doing. When rescue crews tried to save these men from the flaming water, it was found that one out of every three was already dead.

The ARIZONA's tattered battle flag and Admiral Kidd's personal two-star flag were framed; they presently hang in the Admiral Kidd Officer's Club at the Naval Training Center in San Diego.

Today, the names of the ship's dead are etched on a marble wall on the ARIZONA Memorial astride the hulk of the sunken ship. The ARIZONA became a symbol of the war, and thousands of tourists a year still take navy-launches out to the site. Many still throw Hawaiian flower leis into the water in memory of the men who remain forever entombed in its sunken hull.

Attempts were made to extricate the bodies of the dead from the ARIZONA, but it could not be done for several reasons. First, the bodies had already badly decomposed. Noxious gases from the many decaying bodies made it difficult to free them from entanglement. It had become dangerous for divers to try to descend into the rusty hulk that might collapse around them at any disturbance of the area. Finally, the hull was still oozing oil. It would be a treacherous and risky attempt. The decision was made to entomb the remains of the dead in the ship's hull and make it the ARIZONA Memorial. It stands in Pearl Harbor as a grim reminder of "the day that will live in infamy," so aptly named by President Franklin D. Roosevelt.

Years later, at the invitation of Vice-Admiral Samuel L. Gravely, JR.,USN, Third Fleet commander, I visited the ARIZONA Memorial. Oil still oozed from the hulk of the great battleship. From the white bridge of the-memorial, the outline of the submerged hulk is still visible in the clear water.

Hickam Field and Wheeler Field had both been attacked and strafed. Kaneohe Naval Air Station on the Windward Side of the island also had been attacked. Some died there.

By 9:25 a.m. on December 7, 1941, 18 ships had been sunk, 140 planes shot down, and 2,403 military and civilian people killed, with another 1,178 wounded. All this occurred in just one hour and twenty minutes.

Now, as we steamed into the great destruction of Pearl Harbor, the crew of the YORKTOWN stood glum and silent on the flight deck. We could not speak. We did not know what to say. There was nothing to say. This could not happen to the U.S. Navy, but it did. We were at war.

The attack on Pearl Harbor was planned by Admiral Isoroku Yamamoto, commander of the Japanese combined fleet. It was his brain-child from the beginning. He knew America, for he had studied at Harvard and had been a naval attache´ in Washington, D.C., and in

England. He knew our strengths and weaknesses and feared the industrial might of the United States and that of the U.S. Navy.

Yamamoto felt that if Japan were to subdue America he would have to cripple the U.S. fleet for at least a year, thus giving Japan time for conquest. If this could not be done, he felt Japan would lose the war, because he knew the industrial capability of the United States. He felt so strongly about this plan of action that he threatened to resign his commission if the Imperial staff did not go along with it.

Often, as a Christian, I have wondered how history might have been changed if the church would have witnessed to the young Yamamoto and won him to Jesus Christ while he was a student or attache´ in America. Such thoughts came much too late, but since that time I have tried to encourage American Christians to bring foreign students into their circles of influence and evangelization.

The Japanese army under General Hideki Tojo, had gained control of Japan's government and was the ruling party. The navy had little opportunity to advise, but upon Yamamoto's threat of resignation, Tojo and the army finally agreed to the admiral's overall plans for the surprise attack on Pearl Harbor. What initially seemed like a victory for the Japanese turned out to be their undoing, for Yamamoto had been right about the industrial and military might of the United States. At Pearl Harbor, the sleeping giant awoke and rose up to conquer its resource-poor attackers.

As we manned the rail entering Pearl Harbor, we realized this was the moment of truth. The crew matured in that moment, as teenage sailors became men and young men attained a stronger stature. We were all men-regardless of age...for we had come face to face with the realities of the war. The USS YORKTOWN and her crew were ready to do battle.

Why the War Occurred

An ordinary military man in the ranks need, not know particularly why wars start nor even how or when they might end. His job is simply to carry out his orders once they are given. When civilian rule and negotiations break down among governments, war ensues. In a sense, war is another phase of diplomacy, albeit a violent one. Horrible as the conflicts may be, the reasons for war can be interesting, particularly in the case of Japan. I shall list several here, although this may appear some what simplistic, and by no means, is it all inclusive.

1. An officer caste had sprung up in the Japanese military, separate from the civil populace, and had taken preeminence.

2. In the American Great Depression beginning in 1929, we levied tariffs on Japanese goods because they were inundating the American economy with cheap products.

3. In the 1930's, Japan invaded and devastated China and committed some of the most brutal atrocities known to man. I personally have seen photographs taken by American sailors who served in the Navy's Asiatic Fleet. These were pictures of the Japanese occupation of Manchuria—"The Rape of Nanking." Japanese soldiers impaled Chinese women on sharp bamboo poles and left them to die. Both men and women lay dead in the streets. They had cruel and inhuman forms and methods of torture, such as running wooden splinters under the fingernails or pulling out the fingernails.They seemed unemotional and heartless in their barbaric conduct. This was the enemy we would have to fight and defeat.

4. The American gunboat PANAY had been bombed.

5. The U.S. had cut Japan's access to raw materials and scrap iron, which crimped their production goals.

6. The oil embargo was imposed. Japan had no natural

resources for many of its needs, so she imported all raw materials and then manufactured for export. If her imported raw materials were curbed, she would be bankrupt.

7. Japan's alliance with Nazi Germany posed a serious threat.

8. The Yamato race produced the emperor and embraced emperor worship. The imperial throne dated back 2,600 years. The Japanese considered themselves to be a master race, much as the Germans did.

9. Japan decided to "free" all European Asiatic colonies by the use of force.

The U.S. immediately declared martial law in Hawaii. There was little Japanese-American treachery in the islands, although there were spies in the Japanese consulate. There was, however, much suspicion even though, for the most part, Japanese Americans were loyal to the United States. This was an extremely difficult time for Japanese Americans both in Hawaii and on the Mainland, but we had never faced Asiatic aggression before and were, therefore, suspicious of all Asians, often unjustifiably so.

We were at war!

Chapter Five

Battle of the Coral Sea

The USS YORKTOWN with its task force sailed out of Pearl Harbor on February 16, 1942. It was the flagship of TF-17, with Rear Admiral Frank Jack ("Blackjack") Fletcher in command. Sailing with the YORKTOWN were the Cruisers ASTORIA and LOUISVILLE, the Oiler GUADALUPE, and the Destroyers SIMS, ANDERSON, HAMMAN, and WALKE—eight ships in all. We headed south and east toward the Coral Sea, the ocean that lies off the Great Barrier Reef on the coast of Australia, about 5,000 miles from Hawaii. We were angry and ready to do combat after witnessing the shameless destruction at Pearl Harbor.

Japan had designs on Australia. We believed their plan was to seize Port Moresby and establish an outpost on New Guinea, from which they could launch an invasion of the Australian continent. They also planned to close and control the shipping lanes to Australia and, in so doing, cut and strangle Australia's economic lifeline. To accomplish this, they would have to annihilate or at least neutralize the U.S. fleet; our presence was foiling the Japanese plans.

As we approached the area, YORKTOWN's Task Force 17 joined that of the carrier USS LEXINGTON, flagship for TF-11, to form one large battle group. Several engagements ensued, with attacks on Lae and Salamaua, Port Moresby, Tulagi, and Bougainville. There was no question then that we were at serious war and unleashing the previously untried power of the U.S. Navy on enemy targets.

Although we did not know it, we were preparing for the Battle of the Coral Sea, which would result in serious naval losses for Japan. The losses of ships they would sustain, at this point, would later result in the greatest naval losses in history, which would occur in the Battle of Midway. Up to this point, the Japanese had been arrogant and abusive, but this would soon change.

The Calm Before the Storm

In March, fresh provisions had run low, and we were once again eating a lot of beans and spaghetti. This had become commonplace, and men accustomed to a peacetime navy began to complain. The chaplain, Lieutenant Commander Frank Hamilton, had a bright idea. He staged a "Jamboree" on April 10 to stir up some fun and excitement.

A big T-bone steak—called "the only one in captivity"—was auctioned off. A mess attendant carried the steak in a glass cage on the flight deck for all to see, guarded by four U.S. Marines with fixed bayonets. Our band marched, playing Sousa's marches while they paraded the steak around on the flightdeck. Everyone wanted a bite of that steak, but those who won were Said, storekeeper second class; H. Brown, coxswain; P.C. Serwanski, musician first class; Montgomery, seaman second class; and Kord, seaman second class.

Following the auction, a "smoker" (any type of entertainment put on by the crew) was scheduled. Chief Electrician Mate Walter Fox held the crew spellbound with some acts of hypnotism. He was entertaining, and a lot of fun to watch. Chief Fox conducted a class on hypnotism and hypnotized some crew members. He gave one sailor an onion and told him when he ate it, it would taste like an apple. The lad ate it in front of the group and acted as if he were eating one of the finest apples he had ever tasted. When Fox snapped him out of it, he was amazed to find he was eating an onion.

Fireman Third Class Sid Flum and Seaman Second Class Pete Montalvo jitterbugged for our entertainment. The YORKTOWN orchestra, considered the best in the fleet, played swing tunes. It was fun and broke the monotony of steaming.

The YORKTOWN Band Number 6, were all graduates from the U.S. Navy School of Music in Washington, D.C. Lieutenant Commander Charles Benter, USN, the conductor of the U.S. Navy Band, had established the school to bring in fine musicians from the high schools across the nation. They were trained in music harmony, theory, and composition and instructed on their instruments. Many hours of practice went into their training. Commander Benter's plan was to provide and promote better bands in the fleet.

The band was made up of the following men: Trumpets: T.E. Lloyd, R.C. Cady, F.L. Thompson, and J.G. Seymour; Clarinets: S.E. Linzey, F.J.Baldino, W.G. Smith, P.C. Serwanski, and H.C. Fogle; Trombones: Emil Kimmel, P.R. Kocker, and A.W. Porter; Baritone: Austin Groves; French Horns: C.E. Foster and H.A.

Hoffman; Basses: W.B. Joneson and R.H. Zander; Drums: H.C. Stein and G.P. Weiser; Flute: G.L. Roop; and Bandmaster: E.L. Oakley.

H.C. (Sammy) Stein was conceded to be one of the finest drummers in the fleet. R.H. Zander and A.W. Porter were arrangers and composers. It was a great team, and I was proud to be a part of it.

The Deacon

The ship's chaplain, Lieutenant Commander Frank R. Hamilton, held Divine Services on board each Sunday. Before the war and in those early days, Divine Services were generally a formal affair, and the men were compelled to attend in uniform. Because of this, not many men were attracted to the chaplain's services.

Under the chaplain's sponsorship, I was permitted to perform the duties of a lay leader and organize a weekly Bible study for men of all Christian faiths.We were informal, and the men could attend in dungarees. We began with nine men and reached a peak number of 63 per service. I quickly attained the title "the Deacon."

In our group we sang the old favorite hymns that most men from the historic churches knew in 1942. In addition to our Bible studies, we encouraged testimonies of personal triumphs and answers to prayer, took prayer requests, and prayed together each week. A real Christian brotherhood was formed in those final days before our first great battle. Many years later, when I became Command Chaplain on board the carrier, USS CORAL SEA, I recalled the Bible study I initiated and conducted on our way to that historic confrontation would be the start of my long navy career of leading men in worship and Christian experience.

To the best of my ability, I made myself available to counsel with men about their problems and anxieties.

This gave me the opportunity to lead many to Christ. To be able to minister effectively, I dedicated much of my free time to the study of the Bible by taking the Berean Correspondence Courses provided by the Assemblies of God. My driving passion was **2 Timothy 2:15,** *"Study to show thyself approved unto God, a workman that needeth not to be ashamed, rightly dividing the word of truth."*

It was good fellowship and a cohesive group, and this gave us the opportunity to be witnesses to the ship's company. Often, when we went ashore in small boats, from the ship at anchor, I would hand out gospel tracts to the men as they came off the boats.

We held our meetings weekly in one of the pilots' ready-rooms. The ready-rooms were used to brief the pilots for flight operations. They were comfortable, had leather chairs, and were air-conditioned. We were grateful to the Chaplain, who had helped us obtain the use of these facilities.

In those days, enlisted personnel had no "rights" as we speak of them today. We did as we were told and kept our mouths shut. Often Christians in the Navy were looked down on or given little respect, but we decided to take a stand for our Lord.

On one occasion, I was denied promotion to musician first class because of my religious stance and testimony. There were no opportunities to appeal, no rights, nor would I complain; it was worth everything to be a Christian.

One night I approached a veteran chief petty officer in the squadron to get the keys to the flight ready-room to conduct our Bible study. "Chief," I said, "I'm 'the Deacon.' I want the key to the ready-room. We have Bible study tonight."

I guess he thought he would have some fun with a young sailor. "You want what?" he bellowed out loudly for all to hear. He was intimidating.

I believe it was the Holy Spirit who prompted me to reply to him just as raucously. I yelled back loud and clear, "I want the keys to the ready-room for Bible study tonight, Sir!"

He must have thought that I was angry. He mellowed quickly and grumbled, "Okay, okay! All right!" That was a small victory for me and the group.

In Port at Tonga

We had been at sea for 63 days and fresh provisions in the ship were running low, so on April 20th we were ordered into Tongatabu in the Tongan Islands to replenish the ship. The Japanese apparently did not realize we were using the port, for we took on 578 tons of stores from the stores ship BRIDGE.

We anchored in Nukualofa Harbor, a beautiful deep water port. The big Queen of Tonga had sent the native girls into the hills while the Navy was in port to keep them away from our sailors. There were no alcoholic beverages to be bought, for they had been banned and outlawed on Tonga. The islands were dry.

The Tongan Islands are a small group of tropical islands 2,000 miles northeast of Sydney, Australia. Tongatabu was the leading island and the capital. It was and is a true kingdom that never has been a colony or protectorate of any European or American nation. It had lush vegetation and grew the finest coconuts, papayas, and bananas anywhere in the world.

The band played a concert in the park one day, and we played Sousa's marches and some semi-classical numbers. The Tongans showed no emotion, reaction, nor appreciation for our music. We could not tell whether or not they liked it.

Finally, out of desperation the bandmaster, Chief Musician Oakley, told us to break out a novelty number called "The Big Bass Drum." Not much music, mostly noise, with lots of cymbal crashes, drum beats, and syncopated rhythm.

On the first cymbal crash by musician George Weiser, the crowd cheered and yelled. This kept up all through the whole piece. They loved it. Now we knew what to play, and we gave them a good concert.

The Tongan people were devout Christians, having been converted by Wesleyan missionaries over a century before. I was soon to find that the church played a major role in their personal lives.

One day I went ashore and met a Tongan man with his son riding in a buckboard wagon drawn by a mule. I hailed him, and he stopped. I told him I wanted some papayas, coconuts, and bananas, so he got out of the wagon and led me through a cluster of women and children among the palms. This, I found, was a native school. When we came to his hut, another son got the fruit for me. This lad took a running start and literally ran up to the top of a 50-foot coconut palm that was leaning at a 45-degree angle and threw coconuts down to us. He was nimble and agile.

After thanking him, I tried to make arrangements to return to see him on the following Sunday. Language was a barrier, but when he realized that I was trying to tell him I wanted to return and visit him on Sunday, he clouded up and with a disapproving look said in a very serious manner, "No! Me go to church!"

Noting his intense sincerity, I asked, "Are you a Christian?"

On hearing the word, "Christian," he grinned and replied, "Yes, me Christian."

When I told him that I was a Christian, he said in Pidgin English, "Dot's goot," and stuck out his hand to shake mine.

Despite the language barrier, we managed to communicate and set a date when I could come over to visit him at his sister's hut for a meal.

On the appointed day I met the new friend, and we had a dinner of fruits and nuts, an unusual meal for me. We ate and enjoyed a mutual sense of Christian fellowship with few words being exchanged between us. While we had a language barrier, there was no hindrance to our spiritual fellowship.There was a felt bond of kinship between us.

When I got ready to leave, he presented me with a beautiful tapa cloth his sister had made especially for me. Tapa cloths are made from the inner bark of the tapa tree. The bark is stripped from the tree and beaten out by the men into strips. They are formed together and made into sheets to be used for curtains, bed rolls, table cloths, and, in some cases, loin cloths for the men. After the men have beaten out the bark into the cloth, the women apply the coloration and designs. They make great gifts and souvenirs from Tonga.

The tapa cloth presented to me was about three feet square with a pattern of green and black dyes forming margins around the edges. Across the diagonal in black were drawn the Tongan words, "OFA-ATU."

As he handed me the cloth, he looked me in the eyes and said, "You Christian. Me Christian. OFA-ATU—I love you."

I was amazed at the Tongan's concept of Christian love. We hardly express our love to one another like this in America. I gratefully accepted it and thanked him. Our stay in Tonga was wonderful, but much too short.

The day our ship left port, my Tongan brother accompanied me to the pier. His clothes were well worn, and he always wore an old straw hat. As the YORKTOWN pulled away from the pier, I saw him making his way to church, again—a custom the Tongan Christians hold sacred.

As the distance began to separate us, I could see him no longer but his words, OFA-ATU, kept ringing in my ears. OFA-ATU—I love you.

We had a good visit and a respite from war-time patrol, but now it would be back to business as usual. On April 27, it was back to sea and the war.

The Battle of the Coral Sea

The raid at Tulagi on March 3 and 4 had been disastrous for the Japanese. They had been bent on taking Port Moresby in New Guinea and establishing an outpost from which they would be in position to invade Australia. Such was the plan, but it was not to be.

Our air group had sunk eight or nine ships at Tulagi and damaged others. Until this time, the Japanese did not know of our location. In fact, for a time, they did not seem to be aware that we were in the Coral Sea. The Aircraft Carriers YORKTOWN and LEXINGTON had joined forces to check their movements.

Naval battles do not last long, usually only for minutes, but time is required to locate enemy forces and jockey into position for superiority. This procedure went on for nearly a week in the Coral Sea. However, in those days, we did not have the modern equipment the Navy has today. Much observation was done by scouting planes and the visual sightings of lights at night. We did have the "bed-springs" radar on the mast, but the Japanese had no radar at all.

The first contact with the Japanese fleet came on May 7th. The two fleets were in close proximity, only 30 miles apart and playing hide and seek. On this date, Japanese aircraft sank the Oiler NEOSHO and the Destroyer SIMS. The NEOSHO had refueled both the YORKTOWN and the LEXINGTON before it was sunk thirty-six hours later. The Japanese apparently thought it was an aircraft carrier because they bombed it. NEOSHO was left a floating derelict, drifting for four days before she was located by the Destroyer HENLEY, which sank the charred hulk with a couple of torpedoes and rescued fourteen of crewmen from the sunken SIMS. On the NEOSHO, 176 crewmen were immediate fatalities. Another 68 men abandoned ship on life rafts tied together, but when they were located ten days later only four were still alive. They were rescued by the Destroyer HELMS.

In six or seven minutes of intense attack, the YORKTOWN's air group sank the Japanese aircraft carrier SHOHO, resulting in the loss of about 500 Japanese seamen.

War is a terrible thing, but even in war funny things happen, made more intensely humorous by the extreme seriousness of the moment. That evening six Japanese aircraft got in our landing pattern and attempted to fly aboard the YORKTOWN, thinking we were their ship. When it became apparent they were not our planes, we opened fire and they flew off. One plane already had his tailhook down ready to catch the cable and land when we fired on him. The pilot shook his fist at us as he sped away.

By midnight, the fleets had separated and temporarily lost contact with each other; but we had the ominous feeling that the next day, May 8th, would be the showdown. Enemy forces, theirs and ours, had found each other.

It was just about dawn on the morning of May 8th when the Japanese fleet sent out scouts to look for the U.S. task force. At about 8:15 a.m. our own scouts spotted the Japanese ships, and at 11:00 a.m. our planes were ordered to attack the Japanese.

The Battle of the Coral Sea was unlike anything that had ever occurred before, it was the first naval battle ever fought in which the surface ships never saw each other. It was the first naval battle to be fought entirely with aircraft.

Attack on the YORKTOWN

A scout plane from the LEXINGTON spotted a fifteen to sixteen ship Japanese task force comprised of two carriers, five cruisers, and several destroyers. A scout plane from the YORKTOWN then spotted a second task force made up of one battleship, two carriers, six heavy cruisers, and four destroyers. These forces were 180 miles away.

I was an enlisted musician, but during battle the ship's band does not sit on the deck in concert formation playing "Nearer, My God to Thee" while the ship goes down, though that possibility may be nearer than one thinks. Bandsmen have various duties in times of battle. Some work as medical corpsmen and stretcher bearers, working with the ship's doctor. Others, such as I, were telephone talkers at various repair parties. Musician W.G. Smith was a telephone talker at Central Battle Station. I was the telephone talker for Repair Party 4, located on the third deck amid ships in the galley compartment. It was my job to report messages from the officer at Central Battle Station in the bowels of the ship, to my repair party officer, Warrant Officer B.M. McKensie. I also had to relay his messages and replies back to Central Station.

Repair parties are located throughout the ship to assess and repair damage to the ship in their localities so they can keep the ship afloat and steaming. They fight fires, shore up bulkheads, patch holes, keep firefighting equipment operating, keep electrical systems operable, and the like. Doctors or medical corpsman in the area take care of the wounded.

Prior to the battle, I thought the task would be nearly impossible, because I had to remember frame numbers and hatch numbers plus other commands back and forth. No mistakes were allowed. However, once the battle began, I was surprised at how easily it came after all the training and practice.

During a battle, the men lie or sit on the deck. If they were to stand up they could break their necks on the overheads if the ship were to lurch violently due to explosions. It seemed the British had this experience and passed it on to us.

As the battle developed, we were lying down on the third deck, which was right at water level and a prime target for torpedo strikes. I had the headphones on. All of a sudden I heard the man on the bridge announce over the phones, "Enemy aircraft approaching 100 miles." A short time later, the voice said, "Enemy aircraft approaching 50 miles." Then, he said, "Stand by for torpedo attack."

At once a strange feeling or sensation came over me, a strange awareness of reality. It seemed like an eerie consciousness of the moment of truth. I wondered if this could be real. Up to this moment, we had played war. We had rehearsed battle plans. We had actually bombed others. But now, at any moment, the decks could explode beneath me, and that would be the end for many, including me. This was not a practice run.

As I lay on the deck in advance of the impending event, I tried to imagine what it would be like. In my mind's eye I could see the planes approaching. How would it feel to be blown to bits. In a split second, I could be in eternity. How would that feel? Where is eternity? Is it going to happen? How do I know? When? What would it be like to meet God? It could happen now, at any moment. Random thoughts go through one's mind at a time like that. I was a born-again Christian and ready to meet the Lord, but I was young and human, too. A situation such as this readily concentrates the mind.

We waited, but not for long.

Seventy Japanese torpedo planes had been sent to attack LEXINGTON and YORKTOWN. As the torpedo planes made their run on YORKTOWN, God was merciful. Not only that, but we had an excellent skipper in Captain Elliott Buckmaster.

The YORKTOWN's own bombers and torpedo planes had gone flying against the enemy ships and aircraft. The ship's defense against the enemy torpedo planes and bombers was the concerted action of the ship's anti-aircraft guns and the Combat Air Patrol (CAP), composed of fighter planes that fly overhead to interdict approaching enemy aircraft. So, while I was lying on the third deck with my earphones on, the ship's guns and CAP planes were fighting for our lives and their own.

Torpedo planes launch their torpedoes at the broadside of a ship to blow the side out and thereby sink it. To avoid such action the captain turns his ship into the torpedoes so as to give them less area to hit and hopefully evade them. This is what Captain Buckmaster did, and he pulled it off.

Captain Buckmaster had been a destroyer skipper as a junior officer and in the Battle of the Coral Sea he handled the large carrier as if it were a small destroyer. He made a hard turn to port to dodge torpedoes.When a ship makes a hard turn, it lists or leans in the opposite direction. Immediately, on making a hard starboard turn the carrier did not even come out of the list. Instead, it banked the turn to starboard. In spite of its huge size, the YORKTOWN dodged and missed all the torpedoes the Japanese launched at us.

But it was not over.

We wondered where the bombers were.

In a coordinated naval air attack, bombers and torpedo planes usually attack simultaneously or nearly so. Torpedoes come from the side and the bombs come from high overhead. If the ship concerns itself only with the bombs coming from overhead, the torpedoes will get it; and if the ship concerns itself with the torpedoes alone, the bombs will likely get through. But for some reason, and surely a tactical mistake, the Japanese air group was not coordinated, which turned out to be good for us.

Then, over the phones from the bridge, came, "Enemy aircraft approaching. Stand by for air attack."

Lying on the deck with my earphones on, I wondered if we would get through this one. The torpedoes missed, but what would the bombs do? Again, I tried to imagine how it would be. We still escaped the experience of being hit. Would it happen? Would a bomb drop right on my repair party? Would it rip up the deck? Would fires break out? Could we handle it? I had seen the destruction at Pearl Harbor, and the vision of torn and twisted ships was still fresh in my mind.

Again the thought came, "This could be the end." I was only twenty-one years old and married for only nine months. I had a lovely wife at home. I wanted to return to her. Will it be? For then, I had to lie on the deck and take it.

There had been a little time between the torpedo and bombing attacks, so we had a little breather. We were served candy bars for lunch to give us energy, since we had no time to eat a meal.

Musician G.L. Roop said to me, "Deacon, I've been doing some praying."

I replied, "Don't feel alone, Mate. Many of us are praying."

At about 11:30 a.m. it happened.

The bombers came, and the bombs dropped. There were six near misses. Some explosions pierced the side of the ship in several places, and some dented the skin of the hull below the waterline.

Then—WHAM!

A direct hit on the flight deck ripped through thick metal like it was paper, throwing us about our compartment and sending shrapnel flying through our steel bulkhead. The bomb tore through to five decks below and exploded. It had gone through the compartments where the Marines lived and continued down through Repair

Party 5, the group just forward of Repair Party 4, where I was located.

This was an armor-piercing shell, which tore through the decks. Steel decks were no barrier to it. One report was that 30 compartments had been gutted. It left a gaping hole in the third deck, the one we were on, just forward of us in the next compartment. We were separated from the blast only by one bulkhead (steel wall) and a water-tight door, and it was punctured by the steel debris that had crashed through it.

Bulkheads were damaged, water-tight doors were blown off their hinges, and fires were burning in the stores compartments. Smoke filled our section of the ship.

Electric cables had been severed, so we were in complete darkness. One injured man burst through the water-tight door between us and the destruction and cried out, "My God, we've been hit!" Then he fell to the deck. The medics took him to the sick bay for treatment.

Three of the ship's boilers were put out of commission, but our engineers got us back on line in about 30 minutes.

Forty-five or fifty men were immediately killed, and many more were seriously wounded. Some men were disintegrated against the bulkheads by the blast. Others were injured and burned. I saw big men, good men, real men, cry that day. It was not a cry of fear but of grief. One need not be ashamed to cry. Men lost shipmates with whom they had served for years, and I joined them.

Most of Repair Party 5 was wiped out, and the dead were laid out on the mess decks to await burial at sea. Just after midnight the next day, the chaplain held the burial-at-sea ceremony; and as the dead were put over the side in weighted canvas bags, he committed them to the deep.

Had that one bomb fallen only a few feet abaft (sternward from) Repair Party 5, it would have fallen on my Repair Party 4, and we would have been the ones to suffer the casualties.

Planking was placed over the hole in the compartment so we could walk back and forth to carry out our duties. The pungent smell of burnt flesh, sweet and nauseous, was sickening. Every time we had to go through the compartment we had to cover our mouths and noses to avoid breathing it, for it was so penetrating and repulsive.

The Sinking of the LEXINGTON

The USS LEXINGTON was not so fortunate, for in just four minutes she had received two torpedoes and two bomb hits. Being a much heavier ship, apparently she could not make the necessary turns as rapidly as did theYORKTOWN. She was afire from stem to stern—a mass of flames her crew could not control. Aviation fuel lines had broken, and the fuel kept feeding the fire. Explosion after explosion racked the ship until, finally, Admiral AubreyW. Fitch advised the ship's captain, Frederick G. Sherman, to abandon ship.

As the commanding officer and his executive officer went down the lines to the water, according to one report, they were both blown off the lines by another explosion. Cruisers and destroyers came alongside the LEXINGTON and took men aboard from the ship and the water.

The temperature of the Coral Sea water around the ship was about 90 degrees—hot and oily. Due to explosions, there were no sharks in the area. Thankfully, there was no fire on the sea.

Henry ("Hank") Johnson, a photographer third class, had been taking motion pictures on the flight deck of the LEXINGTON. He ran out of film, so he went below to the photo lab to get fresh film for his Bell and Howell camera. At that moment, the LEXINGTON received a direct bomb hit on the forward elevator. The galley was next door to the photo lab. The bomb burst large steam pipes overhead, which spewed out live steam under great pressure, blowing off Hank's shirt and searing his face and shoulder.

"The pain was unbearable," he told me in our interview fifty-four years later. He was sent to sick bay and treated for burns and shock, but he kept at his work. Tannic acid was applied to his burnt face and shoulder to lessen the pain and prevent infection. It would form a skin for his burnt flesh.

The ship also had been torpedoed and listed heavily, putting it out of action. Destroyers came alongside to remove the seriously wounded. Those destroyers bumped and banged angrily against the hull of the LEXINGTON in the choppy seas. It seemed disaster was imminent. Finally, Captain Sherman, the commanding officer, ordered, "Abandon ship!"

Hank told me, "I could not believe it! I could not believe it!"

"This ship is going to blow," said the captain. And later that night it did blow with a great and final explosion.

Hank obeyed and went over the side about midships. He told me,"Sailors began going over the side of the LEXINGTON down cargo nets. We removed our clothing down to our shorts. I dropped into the water, and my face and shoulder began to hurt terribly in the salty brine. Oh, it hurt! My face was raw. Then, once I was in the water, I could not get away from the hulking ship. I would try to swim away, and the waves would bash me back against the side of the ship."

In his weakened condition, Hank was struggling for his very life. In great pain and shock, his strength almost gone, he felt he could not take it any longer. He felt like giving up. "I didn't think I was going to make it," he said.

He was trying to get away from the sinking ship, because if it sank rapidly, it could form an eddy or whirlpool and take a person down like a vacuum.

But God was merciful. In far away Virginia, Hank had a Spirit-filled Christian sister, Esther Sandahl, who several hours prior to the battle was praying in the Spirit. She and her husband Arthur had been Assemblies of God missionaries in China and in Kuala Lumpur in Malaysia.

She knew nothing of her brother's condition or that he was in danger, for news of the battle had not been published. Yet, she felt a compulsion to pray—an urgent call to intercessory prayer. She did not know for what, but she began to pray in the Spirit and continued for about four or five hours until she felt that God had heard and answered her prayer. She had heeded the command of the apostle Paul when he said in **Romans 8:26-27:** *"Likewise the Spirit also helpeth our infirmities: for we know not what we should pray for as we ought:but the Spirit itself maketh intercession for us with groanings which cannot be uttered. And he that searcheth the hearts knoweth what is the mind of the Spirit,because he maketh intercession for the saints according to the will of God."*

Esther Sandahl felt a burden for prayer and prayed in the Spirit for several hours without knowing why. She prayed until she felt the victory, or, as the Holiness people used to say, until she "prayed through." She then felt a relief and release in prayer. She knew nothing of her brother's danger or even of the battle. She did not know he was in the water struggling for his very life.

At that precise moment when his sister felt victory, the sailor in the oily sea mustered all the strength he had left and with the effort of his life got clear from the sinking LEXINGTON. It was then that he received the answer to his sister's prayers. He said, "I was about to give up, but all of a sudden somebody threw me a line. A boat towed me over to the Cruiser MINNEAPOLIS, and they hoisted me aboard. I was going to make it!"

In the sick bay the next day, a doctor examined his burns. The doctor said, "All right, lie down." Hank said he does not remember the doctor giving him an anaesthetic to relieve the pain, but with his scalpel he began to scrape and slice away the burnt skin and flesh from his raw face and shoulder. Hank said, "Blood ran all over the place, and the pain was severe." Then the doctor sprayed on a "brilliant green spray," which was a new treatment for burns at that time. The result: no scars when he healed.

Years later, when I spoke with him I said, "Hank, you were fortunate."

"Yes, I was," he said. "Somebody up there was watching over me."

God has His own communications system. The sailor was losing his life, injured and helpless in the water. In distant Virginia, God moved his sister in the Spirit, who knew how to pray in the Spirit, and she moved the hand of God. He heard and answered her prayer and saved her brother from the sea.

Henry ("Hank") Johnson was the eighth of ten children—five boys and five girls. The five boys served in the Navy during World War II. Their mother Cecelia Johnson and his sister Esther (Johnson) Sandahl prayed daily for them that God would spare them and return them safely home.

The LEXINGTON sank that day, but not immediately. Because she was burning fiercely and brightly, she was illuminating the whole area, thus making the rest of us a target in the night. So Admiral Jack Fletcher ordered the Destroyer PHELPS to fire four torpedoes into the burning aircraft carrier. The ship sank stern first, and slid into the sea. Captain Buckmaster was deeply affected by this sight, for he had previously served as executive officer on board the LEXINGTON. Out of a crew of 3,000 on the aircraft carrier, about 200 men died.

We lost three ships in the Battle of the Coral Sea: the Carrier LEXINGTON, the Destroyer SIMS, and the Oiler NEOSHO. But we sank the Japanese carrier SHOHO and damaged two other large carriers, the SHOKAKU and the ZUIKAKU. These carriers had to return to Japan for repairs, which kept them out of the Battle of Midway one month later. Had they been able to take part in that battle, it could well have altered the outcome for us.

God was in control. He had intervened in the Battle of the Coral Sea, and we would see His hand again at Midway.

Psychologically, this greatly affected the Japanese, for it altered their plans for conquest. The Port Moresby campaign never came off. To save face, Admiral Yamamoto had to avenge himself on the U.S. fleet. At all costs, he felt compelled to find and destroy the American aircraft carriers he had missed in the Pearl Harbor attack.

Back to Pearl Harbor

We left the Coral Sea and began to make our way back to Pearl Harbor via Tongatabu. We were leaving an oil slick in our wake due to leaking fuel tanks on the port side. We would be glad to see Tonga again.

While at sea, on our way to Tongatabu, a damage control party from the Cruiser USS PORTLAND came aboard one day to study our damage control procedures and to see how effectively we had sustained and contained our damage. This would provide an on-site lesson for that crew.

The group had come over in a ship's boat and had come up the accommodation ladder that had been rigged. I was with the YORKTOWN party that greeted them. They came up the ladder on the side of the ship.

When they reached the hangar deck, I noticed that one of the sailors had a Gideon New Testament in the top pocket of his white uniform. I sidled up to him and asked, "Are you a Christian?"

"Yes, I am," he replied. "I've been a Christian for only a week."

"Do you have a Bible study group in the PORTLAND?" I queried.

"No, I'm the only Christian in the ship," he sadly commented. The cruiser had a thousand men on board.

"That can't be so," I said. "When you get back to the ship, start a Bible class. Be a witness for Jesus Christ. Get men saved, and get many more back into fellowship."

We had a Bible class in the YORKTOWN that met a couple of nights each week under my leadership.

The sailor continued. "I need some Bibles." I went below and came up with a carton of fifty New Testaments that had been provided to us by the Gideon Society. "Get them out," I said. "And we'll pray for you."

After showing this group the effects of the bomb and fire and how we had controlled the damage, the party left the ship and returned to the PORTLAND. We said our "Goodbyes" and waved them off.

I began to pray that he would be successful in organizing and leading a Bible study in the PORTLAND. "I had no idea the Lord would send me to the ship a month later to organize the group; and that years later a mother would testify to her son's accepting Christ due to our efforts."

We arrived in Tonga, and very shortly after Admiral Chester W. Nimitz ordered the YORKTOWN back to Pearl Harbor. When we entered Pearl Harbor, we had been at sea for 104 days except for our short stay in Tongatabu. YORKTOWN had become the "Waltzing Matilda."

Over the side...Men from USS LEXINGTON (CV–2) abandon ship by going down the lines into the water when the carrier began to sink. Two bomb hits and two torpedoes hits started uncontrollable fires that doomed the ship.   —Photo courtesy of Henry Johnson Collection, Huntington Beach, CA

Fire gets out of control in the USS LEXINGTON (CV–2). After receiving two bomb hits and two torpedoes the crew makes all efforts to control the fires.   —Photo courtesy of Henry Johnson Collection, Huntington Beach, CA

Abandon ship! Motor whale boats from a nearby U.S. destroyer picks up survivors from USS LEXINGTON (CV–2)   —Photo courtesy of Henry Johnson Collection, Huntington Beach, CA

The USS LEXINGTON (CV–2) is on fire. Having received two bomb hits and two torpedoes from Japanese aircraft. The Battle of the Coral Sea, May 8, 1942. —Photo courtesy of Henry Johnson Collection, Huntington Beach, CA

Fires continue to range in USS LEXINGTON (CV–2). The crew prepares to abandon ship. U.S. scout plane patrols the stricken ship.   —Photo courtesy of Henry Johnson Collection, Huntington Beach, CA

"She's gonna blow!" Unending fires and explosions in the USS LEXINGTON (CV–2) rip the interior of the ship. The fires increased in intensity due to ruptured aviation fuel lines spreading the flames.   —Photo courtesy of Henry Johnson Collection, Huntington Beach, CA

Uncontrollable fire sweeps through the USS LEXINGTON (CV–2). Broken aviation fuel lines continually fuel the flames. —Photo courtesy of Henry Johnson Collection, Huntington Beach, CA

Seamen abandon ship, USS LEXINGTON (CV–2) in the
Battle of the Coral Sea, May 8, 1942. Sailors are moving away
from the stricken ship in a motor whale boat from a nearby
Navy destroyer.   —Photo courtesy of Henry Johnson
Collection, Huntington Beach, CA

Abandon ship! Men go over the side of USS LEXINGTON
(CV–2) and are pulled out of the sea by motor whale boats from
nearby U.S. Navy destroyers. —Photo courtesy of Henry Johnson
Collection, Huntington Beach, CA

Seaman Harry O'Neal Fitzsimmons served in the Navy
Cruiser USS PORTLAND. He was killed in The Battle of
Guadalcanal when the ship took a torpedo strike in the stern
plates on November 12, 1942.   —Photo courtesy Gary
Fitzsimmons, Bakersfield, CA

The Navy Hymn

ETERNAL FATHER, STRONG TO SAVE

Eternal Father, strong save,
Whose arm hath bound the restless wave,
Who bids the mighty ocean deep
its own appointed limits keep;
O hear us when we cry to Thee
For those in peril on the sea!

(Verse One)

Lord, guard and guide the men who fly
Through the great spaces in the sky,
Be with them always in the air,
In darkening storms or sunlight fair.
O hear us when we lift our prayer
For those in peril in the air!

(Verse Two)

Amen

Chapter Six

Battle of Midway

The YORKTOWN came out of the Battle of the Coral Sea a crippled ship, trailing in her wake a long, glistening oil slick that streamed from her ruptured fuel tanks. The great carrier had dodged nine torpedoes and been shaken by six near bomb misses, but that one armor-piercing bomb had penetrated five decks and destroyed thirty compartments, killing forty-five or fifty men, injuring many others, and damaging or blowing away bulkheads and watertight doors. We may have turned from boys of the peacetime Navy to men at our experience of the catastrophe at Pearl Harbor, but after the Battle of the Coral Sea we were seasoned and serious men of war.

The Meaning of the Coral Sea

We did not have a full report on the Battle of the Coral Sea until we were thousands of miles away and steaming toward Pearl Harbor. The trade-off had not been equal in loss of ships, but strategically it was a success for the U.S. Navy. Japan's drive to the South had been halted, the greater invasion of New Guinea had been put on hold, never to be carried out. Had the SHOKAKU and ZUIKAKU not been damaged in the battle of the Coral Sea, the odds at Midway would have been greater, six Japanese fleet carriers opposed to three American flat tops—the ENTERPRISE, the HORNET, and the damaged YORKTOWN.

Some historians have acclaimed the Battle of the Coral Sea as the strategic confrontation that changed the course of events for Japan, but the great naval battle—the coup de grace that would turn the tide of the war—took place at Midway Island.

Martin Stephen observed, "Furthermore, Coral Sea— again like Jutland—was a strategic victory even while it was a tactical defeat. For the first time in the war, the Japanese failed to achieve their objectives; they were never to capture Port Moresby, or venture so far south again. For the first time, Japanese forces had retreated; the significance of this in symbolic terms and for the future of Australia was immense." (Stephen, *Sea Battles Close-Up,* page 156) Gordon Prange assessed it, "But strategically speaking, any battle which fails of its purpose cannot be considered a victory, and the Japanese failed to achieve their objective—capture and occupation of Port Moresby. So, considered objectively, it was a draw—a tactical Japanese victory versus a strategic American one." (Prange, *Miracle at Midway,* page 44)

Only 72 Hours

There was something painful about going back into Pearl Harbor. Just over three months before, it was the YORKTOWN that had stood tall and proud while surrounded by the massive destruction of much of the rest of the Pacific fleet; but on May 27, 1942, the YORKTOWN limped into Pearl Harbor underpowered, with one whole section bombed out and trailing oil.

Within hours the ship entered dry dock for repairs to the hull, boilers, engines, watertight doors, and electrical systems. Admiral Chester W. Nimitz—who commanded all the naval operations in the Pacific—personally inspected the ship on its arrival to assess the damage and time needed for repairs.

According to Prange, Nimitz was a courtly and highly-respected Texan. A hard worker, he paid rigorous attention to detail. He was an efficient organizer and conformed to official forms. He was a calm and steady Dutchman who could make ethical judgments. "Here was one of America's great men in the tradition of Robert E. Lee, whom he resembled in temperament, character, and ability." (Prange, page 10) He was not a flamboyant nor gruff sea dog as was Admiral William F. Halsey. Nimitz appeared young for his age, although 57 at the time. His hair had turned white, and he was fair-complexioned with steel-blue eyes.

Captain Elliott Buckmaster, as I remember him, appeared as a harsh, stern man, becoming red-faced when angry. He was a tall man, outspoken or brusque and loud. He was decisive in command, well-trained for his job. He was respected by the officers and men of YORKTOWN, especially since he brought us out the Battle of the Coral Sea having escaped the torpedo attack.

By this time, the ship was badly in need of work. In addition to the war damage from the Battle of the Coral Sea, we had the damage caused by the oil tanker that had scraped our side and had missed the scheduled overhaul we were to have had back at Norfolk, Virginia. The war had thrust us into battle service without full preparation.

Captain Buckmaster requested a six-month overhaul period.

Admiral Nimitz' reply was that he could only give him 72 hours. A major naval confrontation was brewing to the northwest, and the YORKTOWN's presence would be required. Yet, we of the crew were told nothing except that we would sail again in only three days.

Work on the ship commenced at once and continued around the clock. Welders with torches, electricians, and hull technicians swarmed like ants over, around, and under the great ship to try to put us back in battle order.

All liberty had been cancelled on May 26, due to the work that had to be one. However, Admiral Nimitz granted liberty to YORKTOWN personnel because we had been at sea so long (104 days). Many sailors went to the bars on Hotel Street in Honolulu to drink and relax. Some of us attended church to refresh our spirits.

If a man came back on board from liberty having had too much alcohol, the other sailors put him in the showers and sobered him up. He then went on the working party to assist in provisioning ship.

On May 29, just three days later, the YORKTOWN came out of the drydock as scheduled. The hull had been repaired, the third deck had been patched and electrical systems spliced, and the water-tight doors and hatches had been replaced. However, three boilers still were left inoperable because there was not enough time to repair them.

Midway Bound

A few days before we left for Midway, Admiral William F. Halsey came down with a skin rash and had to be hospitalized in Hawaii with the impending Battle of Midway approaching. Admiral Chester W. Nimitz, commander of the U.S. Pacific Fleet, visited him personally in the hospital and asked for his recommendation for his own replacement at Midway. Without hesitation, Admiral Halsey replied, "Raymond A. Spruance." Rear Admiral Spruance was a cruiser admiral, not a flyer. Admiral Nimitz said to Halsey, "But Spruance is not a carrier admiral," to which Halsey responded, "And neither are you!" Nimitz accepted his recommendation and assigned Spruance to command Task Force 16 and the whole operation at Midway. In fact, Spruance went on to became known as one of the greatest naval tacticians.

On May 30, as the YORKTOWN eased out of Pearl Harbor for the last time, our band played "California, Here I Come" as a spoof and a delight to the crew. We all knew better.

We steamed along the Leeward Side of Oahu with its rugged mountains and fringe of palm trees along beautiful beaches. In 1942, it was mostly virgin country with scattered Hawaiian villages and no signs yet of the city of Waianae or the development of the Makaha Valley with its golf courses, apartment complexes, or high-rise hotels. We could not have dreamed then that what the Japanese had failed to do by military conquest they would later accomplish by financial investments and business management. Hawaii was to become the fiftieth state of the United States and a center for international tourism and commerce. In any case, no matter who won or lost the battles of war or peace, the once idyllic paradise of the islands was forever lost to the native Hawaiians who, for decades to come, would seek to understand what had-happened to their Polynesian way of life and their ancestral lands.

It was not until we had left Oahu, passed by Kauai, and were out on the open sea that we were told our destination. We were going to join the fleet at Midway to surprise the next plans of the Japanese. To make the crew feel good and as if to offer a reward for long days and nights at sea, Admiral Nimitz asked the captain to relay a message to us that as soon as the Battle of Midway was over the YORKTOWN would return to the Bremerton Naval Shipyards in Washington State for a complete overhaul period of a year. We all cheered; but it was not to be. The YORKTOWN would never again return home or even again see dry land, for the Battle of Midway was to be her final destination and the ocean bottom her next port of call.

Midway is an island group about 1,150 miles northwest of Honolulu. It is comprised of Easter Island and Sand Island with the surrounding atoll. It was discovered by Americans in 1859; it had no indigenous population. A cable station was opened in 1903, it became a commercial air station of Pan American Airways in 1935, and became a U.S. Navy Base in 1941, thus making it a military target.

The large black albatrosses the Navy called Gooney birds make their home and nests on Midway. They are clumsy birds on land. They can hardly walk because they spend so much time in flight and do not use their legs and feet very much. They waddle because they can hardly walk. Hence, the name Gooney birds. On land, they look "gooney," but in the air they are graceful inflight and fly far out to sea for months at a time. At nesting time, the female lays one egg on the ground, and the male sits on the egg to hatch it. They fly off the island and return to their original nests year after year.

The Gooney birds have caused the Navy much trouble because they stay on the runways and landing strips, thus interfering with flight operations. The Navy moved them once to another island in the Pacific, but when they were released they found their way home and flew right back to Midway.

Yet we on the YORKTOWN never saw Midway. And, as with the Battle of the Coral Sea, we never saw the enemy fleet. Whereas, in earlier days, enemy ships would come at each other broadside and fire their cannons or use grappling hooks at close range, naval battles now were fought by assuming strategic positions, maneuvering against the unseen enemy, and establishing air superiority and attack. We could not have known in 1942 that even this kind of naval warfare would change once more with the greater range of jet aircraft, the coming of nuclear weapons, and the great variety of missiles that would characterize naval operations later in the century.

We Broke Their Code

Commander Joseph Rochefort of Naval Intelligence, with his staff, had broken the Japanese code. From intercepted Japanese messages, he believed the enemy's intention was to attack and take Midway.

To prove this, at Rochefort's insistence, Admiral Nimitz ordered the command at Midway to send out a message saying they were short of water on the island. The Japanese were eavesdropping on our communications, so we hoped they would intercept this one and make a response to it. They did and Rochefort's conclusions were proved correct. We picked up their communications and ascertained by their use of certain code words their plans to invade the islands.

Some historians believe Admiral Yamamoto's plans were to draw the U.S. fleet into open warfare at sea, set the trap, and annihilate it with his superior forces, a cat-and-mouse game. He wished to destroy the carriers he had missed at Pearl Harbor.

Actually, Yamamoto had a two-pronged tactic. He planned a feigned attack on the Aleutian Islands off Alaska as a diversion, hoping Nimitz would take the bait and send his naval forces there. Yamamoto could then make his main attack on Midway, thinking it would be defenseless.

Nimitz did not bite, and Yamamoto did not know we had broken the Japanese code and knew his intentions.

Yamamoto sent sixteen submarines to be on station across the line from Hawaii to Midway to intercept the U.S. fleet in its trek to the north. If he could contain us in

Hawaii, he felt he would have no difficulty in taking Midway without opposition. However, the submarines did not arrive on station until June 3, too late to trap the American fleet. Nimitz had sensed the urgency of the situation and moved the fleet past the picket line before the submarines arrived at their positions. As a result, the Japanese did not know the location of our fleet. When the Battle of Midway began, the Japanese thought we were still in Hawaii.

Midway was to be attacked by opposing Japanese naval forces of 185 ships, 5,000 occupying troops combat ready, and four fleet aircraft carriers that would launch 72 dive bombers, 31 fighters, and 81 torpedo bombers against the U.S. fleet. We would counter this attack with about 25 fighting ships: three carriers, eight cruisers, and fourteen destroyers. The YORKTOWN was to be northeast of Midway and held in reserve due to its crippled condition.

The naval forces converging on Midway were the largest massing of seapower in history. Midway was the greatest and biggest naval battle ever fought to that time. It may be one of the last great naval duels because of the greater range and accuracy of jet aircraft and nuclear missiles.

Actually, those of us on the YORKTOWN never saw the Island of Midway, although I visited the island years later. We sailed northwest to about 200 miles northeast of Midway to await the assault on the island. When we would get the word that it had been attacked, our squadrons were to attack the enemy carriers to either disable them by sinking, or set them on fire to neutralize their air attack.

As far as the Navy could determine, the Japanese did not know we were there. As it turned out, the Navy was right.

We waited.

On the way to Midway, it seemed a spirit of fear hovered over the YORKTOWN like a pall. After all, we had already been in battle, and war was no longer unknown to us. We had felt the heavy lurch of a bomb strike, buried our friends at sea, and seen the horror in the sinking of the LEXINGTON. We knew what was ahead and some of us would likely die. It was an eerie sensation. Some of the pilots had a sense of nervous hilarity due to anxiety. We remembered how Captain Buckmaster had saved our lives by his ability at maneuvering the great ship and avoiding the torpedoes; but now we were under-powered and incapable of such action. Our only hope would be that the battle would end before the Japanese would locate our damaged ship.

We knew it was going to be bad. Just how bad no one could guess, but we knew it was would be worse than the Battle of the Coral Sea. Likely, there would be great loss of life and many injuries.

An Experience in the Spirit

Through all this time the YORKTOWN Bible class was functioning well. Many of us met regularly for Scripture reading, prayers, and fellowship; the numbers were increasing every week. We were from many different churches, but we were all committed Christians and truly ecumenical in spirit. We had a great Christian fellowship.

As the leader of the group, I was still called "the Deacon." Yet, as we moved northward, I became fearful. There was a sense of foreboding throughout the ship, and I was afraid. A terrific paralyzing fear gripped me, animal fear, wild-eyed fear. It held me in its grip like a vice, and I could not shake it. It was smothering me. A spiritual battle was raging in my mind and heart, for we were facing ultimate reality, death and God.

On the night of June 3, as we steamed toward our assigned location northeast of Midway, many sailors could hardly sleep. On the third deck at water-line level. In the darkened compartment, I lay in my bunk on my stomach with my face buried in the pillow. Burdened with apprehension and dread, it seemed like a heavy weight was pressing down on me, and I couldn't shake it off. I lay there alone in the darkness, consumed by my own fear of impending death.

Andy Mikus wrote about the Battle of Midway, "Being on the verge of battle produces mixed psychological emotions. On the one hand, the fear of dying impels one to find safety somewhere. Some will pray or seek the protection of shields of gun positions or even below deck if possible. On the other hand, one's self-respect demands that you do nothing of which to be ashamed later." ("A Clear Day at Midway," *Yorktown Crier,* 1990, No. 4, p. 10)

Finally, in my desperation and mental anxiety I cried aloud to God in my pillow, "Lord, I am saved and I know it. If I must die, then I must. It's okay with me. I'm ready. Only one thing I ask of You, that You take this numbing fear out of my heart and mind so I can do my duty. Amen."

I had thrown myself on the mercy of God.

One of the great benefits of Bible study is by knowing the Scriptures we allow God to use His Word to speak to us. In the first of many times that God would speak to me, He spoke in the words of the prophet Zechariah: *"Not by might, nor by power, but by my spirit, saith the Lord of hosts. "* (**Zechariah. 4:6**)

At that moment, lying face down on my bunk with no one around me and all alone in the dark compartment, as I said "Amen" to my prayer, something wonderful happened. I had an emotional experience I shall never-forget. I sensed...I felt...the weight and pressure of the moment physically and literally lift off my shoulders. At that instant the burden and the fear were dispelled. I could feel it. I was free.

As the psalmist said, *"A thousand shall fall at thy side, and ten thousand at thy right hand; but it shall not come nigh thee."* **(Psalm 91:7)** I had no promise I would be saved from death, but I was assured I would be saved from the fear of death. *"Yea, though I walk through the valley of the shadow of death, I will fear no evil, for thou art with me."* **(Psalm 23:4)**

Meanwhile in San Diego

At that very same moment, Verna had a religious experience comparable to mine.

"I was back in San Diego and knew nothing of the YORKTOWN's impending disaster, the battle, or Stan's experience in prayer. But at this time, about 5,000 miles apart from him, I felt a strange need to pray, not knowing why. I slipped into my bed room and knelt on the floor by the bed and began to weep and pray so emotionally. It was terrible and uncontrollable.

"Dad and Mother Linzey had come to San Diego from Texas to work in the aircraft plants for the duration of the war, and they were living with me. They were nominal Christians but did not know a lot about spiritual warfare.

"They were eating in the kitchen when they heard me weeping in prayer. They did not know how to handle it. People did not groan and pray in the Spirit in their church, nor did they pray a lot. I wondered what they thought of me.

"It was between five and six o'clock in the evening. I began to cry and pray in the Spirit and groan before the Lord in intercessory prayer for over an hour. Finally I felt the victory, or spiritual and mental relief. I felt God had answered my prayer, whatever it was. When Stan and I compared notes later, we found that he and I had been praying at the same moment.

"Jesus said, *'Again I say unto you, That if two of you shall agree on earth as touching any thing that they shall ask, it shall be done for them of my Father which is in heaven.'* **(Matthew 18:19)** We were in agreement in the Spirit.

"We always tried to keep the unity of the Spirit between us. When Stan went to sea, we made a practice of reading the same Scriptures and devotional material on a regular daily basis. We felt this kept us in spiritual harmony with each other and the Lord. "

Out there in rolling seas, in the middle of the Pacific Ocean, I learned that God was at Midway. The Lord had answered my prayer. Through the ensuing battle I felt no fear. I witnessed destruction and saw men die, but I had no fear. Again, as the prophet Isaiah said, *"Thou wilt keep him in perfect peace, whose mind is stayed on thee: because he trusteth in thee."* **(Isaiah 26:3)**

Men turn to God in such times. Lieutenant Jim Gray, skipper of Fighting 6, said, "It is doubtful that there were any atheists in the ENTERPRISE on the night of June 3, 1942." (Walter Lord, *Incredible Victory*, p.87)

In crises times, men's minds have their private thoughts: home, family, children, wives, and community. They become moody, and a spirit of resignation sets in. A nervous gaiety prevails. This had been the mood at Pearl Harbor as well.

The Battle of Midway

The Navy had F4F Wildcats to form the Combat Air Patrol, which hovered over YORKTOWN to protect against invading aircraft. We also had the Dauntless Dive

Bombers. The torpedo planes were the old TBD's (Torpedo Bomber built by Douglas). This was a slow aircraft, it's lack of speed was the cause of the annihilation of the squadrons in the battle. Later in the battle, when one TBD plane dropped his torpedo against one of the Japanese carriers, the torpedo did not explode on impact. Later, when the carrier was sunk by other torpedoes and bombs, Japanese sailors were found clinging to the unexploded American torpedo and using it as a float.

On June 3, our patrol planes spotted the Japanese fleet approaching Midway at about 9:30 a.m., and indeed our fleet was greatly out numbered.

On the morning of June 4, our carriers were standing by in readiness waiting for word that Midway had been attacked, then we would launch our aircraft against their carriers. The Japanese, still did not know we were in the area. At 6:30 a.m., when they began their assault, their first wave of attack was with land bombs on Midway. It was then that Admiral Spruance ordered our aircraft to launch their counterattack. The word came over our loudspeaker, "Midway has been attacked. Launch all aircraft." Off they went—the bombers, the torpedo planes, and the fighters. The Battle of Midway had begun.

As the enemy planes were returning to their carriers to be rearmed and refueled, the Japanese began to have some inkling of the presence of the American fleet. Due to indecision and poor communication from their own scouting planes, they shifted back and forth from bombs to torpedoes. Against proper procedures, they did not stow the bombs, torpedoes, and gasoline tanks as they rearmed their planes but left them lying on the decks. Only then did Japanese Admiral Chuichi Nagumo, commander in chief of the Japanese First Air Fleet, learn of the approaching American aircraft. He ordered his Zero fighters out to intercept them, but it was too late.

In a period of six minutes, American bombers and torpedo planes set three Japanese aircraft carriers ablaze. Our aircraft had caught the enemy carriers with their aircraft on their decks, fuel lines open, bombs and torpedoes lying around their hanger decks, and their flight decks unprotected. At this point, the Japanese found out they were confronting three aircraft carriers instead of none; and we struck them at their most vulnerable moment.

Commander Murr Arnold, the YORKTOWN's air officer, called it a"Godawful lucky coordinated attack." (Robert Cressman, *That Gallant Ship*, page 129) We would rather believe it was the grace of God that saved us that day against numerically superior forces. One of Admiral Spruance's wisest strategies was to withdraw the fleet that night after having destroyed four enemy carriers rather than engaging with the Japanese battleships, or "battlewagons," which would have been disastrous. We had won our objective and turned the tide of the Pacific war.

We realize, of course, that the intelligence and intuition of Admirals Nimitz, Spruance, and Fletcher and their staffs were crucial. But, in war, victory does not always go to the superior forces but to those who make the least mistakes.

The writer of Proverbs said, *"In his heart a man plans his course, but the Lord determines his steps."* **(Proverbs 16:9)** We took calculated risks, but God favored us that day.

Our churches across America had held prayer meetings on our behalf. The President of the United States had inaugurated his Presidential Prayer Breakfasts, and we believe God heard and answered their prayers.

The battle raged hot and heavy, and most of the aircraft were shot out of the sky that day, ours and theirs.

The Sinking of the YORKTOWN

It appeared that YORKTOWN would get away unde-tected and unscathed; but in the afternoon, about 2:00 p.m., enemy planes from the undamaged Japanese carrier HIRYU followed our own planes as they returned to the YORKTOWN and spotted our crippled ship. Our radar picked them up at 46 miles distance heading our way.

All of us ran to our battle stations on the double.

Dog fights clashed over the YORKTOWN as Japanese bombers tried to get through our fighters to the ship.

"Set material condition affirm," said the speaker. That meant close all water-tight doors and hatches against flooding and cut off all ventilation. Put on flash-proof clothing. Enemy planes were coming in.

Again I was at my assigned battle station on the third deck about the water-line level, just like the Battle of the Coral Sea. Memories of that other battle flooded my mind, recollections of little things and of that horrible moment when the bomb blew apart the compartment next to us. I thought of my Verna May...so far away.

"All hands lie down on deck," came the word. I lay down with my headphones on, ready for action.

"Air Department, take cover. Gunnery Department, take cover." The enemy bombers were getting closer.

The only noise to be heard in our compartment was the whine and whir of the engines as the ship picked up speed and began to move this way and that to dodge enemy planes.

The speaker announced, "Stand by for air attack."

Immediately after that announcement, the ship lurched beneath us as three bombs hit the ship, and there were several near misses that shook us hard. One bomb set a fire on the hangar deck and another exploded right in the stack and snuffed out the fires in our boilers, putting them out of commission.

The whining of engines stopped, the YORKTOWN slowed, and we were dead in the water. We were a sitting duck for more air attacks—an ominous and foreboding feeling.

Suddenly, another bomb exploded on the fourth deck below and fore from us, causing another fire.

The third bomb exploded on the flight deck aft of the island structure causing fragment damage to the hangar deck below.

Then the enemy planes were gone, but we knew they would be back. We had been struck by the bombers, but we knew the torpedo planes would soon come.

As we lay dead in the water, the engineers worked feverishly and cross-connected the steam plant (re–routed the steam to make the engines operable);and by 3:40 p.m., we were able to get underway again.

At 3:50 in the afternoon, our radar picked up another enemy air group approaching the ship.

We all knew we had little chance of survival.

The voice said over the loudspeaker, "Stand by for torpedo attack."

We could only make about 15 knots, not nearly fast enough to escape the torpedoes as we did in the Coral Sea.

From my position on the third deck, I could see nothing, but over the headphones I could hear the pro-ceedings above. Looking back on that day, I don't know which would have been better, to hear and know what was going on or to lie there like my friends in the galley compartment without knowing.

I heard the conversation as two Japanese planes got through our air defenses and, in spite of our blazing guns, dropped two torpedoes. They went too deep and missed the ship by passing under the bow.

Then two more planes got through.

I heard the sickening thud as a torpedo struck our ship. It was immediately followed by a second strike. I have never been shot, but I can well imagine it would be similar to what we felt as those torpedoes struck the YORKTOWN. When torpedoes hit a ship, they explode on impact, tearing at the vitals of the ship. They make a tearing or wrenching sensation as they rupture the vessel's innards.

As I lay on the third deck at my station, it felt as if a great arm had lifted the ship out of the sea, shaken it, and dropped it back again. On the drop, seawater flooded into the gaping holes in the hull, and we took a list to the portside of 27 degrees. With such a list, the great ship began to swing in a helpless circle. All our electric lights went out, and broken water mains were pouring water into our compartment as we struggled to survive.

The first torpedo had hit forward on the port side, and the second torpedo hit not far from the same spot. They blew large holes in the carrier's hull that jolted her with great explosions. The generator room had been hit, so all power was lost and electric power failed. The rudder was jammed, and the ship lay dead in the water for a second time. Fuel tanks were ripped open and were pouring oil into the sea.

Some 400 men were dead. Two bandsmen, G.L. Roop and J.G. Seymour, on station in the Post Office compartment, were killed in the explosions. It was said the decks curled up around them. Two weeks before the battle, Musician Charles E. Foster's battle station had been changed from that compartment to the medical station just under the flight deck. He said he felt he owed his life to the divine authority that made the change.

Below decks eerie darkness prevailed throughout the ship. Water mains were broken, and water was flowing over and around us. All lights were out, and smoke filled the compartment. To make matters even worse, with the 27-degree list, all decks and bulkheads were aslant.

The recurring question was: Is the ship going to capsize? We learned later that the ship was listing so heavily that the portside edge of the hangar deck was dipping into the sea.

The commanding officer conferred with his damage control officer, Commander Clarence Aldrich. Fearing the ship might quickly capsize and all hands be lost, Captain Buckmaster gave his last and final order to his crew, a command a sailor never expects to hear: "Abandon ship!"

PSALM 35:1-3

Plead my cause, O Lord, with them that strive with me;
Fight against them that fight against me.
Take hold of shield and buckler,
and stand up for mine help.
Draw out also the spear, and stop the way
against them that persecute me:
Say unto my soul, I am thy salvation.

Chapter Seven

Rescue at Sea

With orders to abandon ship, we now faced the formidable task of finding our way up through the heavily damaged ship. The YORKTOWN had been our home, but we had no intention of letting it become our tomb. There in the darkness, with water gushing about from broken lines, we assumed that many of our friends had been killed. We were grateful to be alive. Only later we learned 400 crew members had died in the torpedo explosions or were drowned in flooded compartments.

Abandoning Ship

There in the galley compartment on the third deck, we knew that to have any chance of survival we would have to climb up the sloping deck, work our way to the bulkhead hatch that now was aslant in the overhead, and repeat the procedure for the decks above. Our great fear was that at any moment the listing ship might capsize or sink three miles to the bottom of the sea. We located our battery-powered battle lanterns and focused all our attention on the single purpose of making our way topside.

Frightened as we might have been, there was no panic. Our navy training took over, and, in the galley compartment, we got in line, to climb up the slippery leaning deck. We took off our shoes to get better footing for our climb and began our ascent. We knew this part of the ship so well we could have located the hatch even without the battle lanterns, but when the first men hesitated we knew that something was wrong.

The water-tight hatch to the second deck was warped shut by the explosions!

However, in the center of each water-tight hatch there was a scuttle, a small circular quick-acting hatch that could be opened by the turn of a wheel. To our great relief, the first man got it open, and the rest of us climbed up through the manhole, each in turn, one at a time. I still look back in amazement as I recall the quiet discipline of the men as we fought for our very lives. The YORKTOWN officers and men were a highly trained and disciplined group.

I remember the hope that rose inside me as my hands grasped the first rungs of the ladder that led me up to the next compartment on the second deck. We then repeated the procedure to arrive at the next level and eventually came out onto the hanger deck—the large, open-sided hanger for our planes just below the top flight deck. My initial joy at seeing daylight was immediately dampened as I gazed in amazement at the sight of the devastation. I saw twisted metal, gaping holes in the steel hangar deck as if a great finger had plucked holes in it, and debris scattered everywhere. Although I had experienced the sloping decks below, this was my first view of the full implications of the 27-degree list to port with the lower edge of the hanger deck often dipping into the water. Near the hatch where I had emerged onto the hangar deck was a totally ravaged fighter plane still tied down to the deck. Amid all this, men were going up, around, and over the debris, and over the side to abandon the derelict ship. The wounded were being dragged across the slippery decks in stretchers, and some were simply picked up and carried bodily.

As I stepped out onto the sloping hangar deck and began to walk across the Number 2 elevator (the lift used to raise or lower the aircraft between the hanger deck and the flight deck), I suddenly lost my footing and began to slide down toward the water on the low side of the hangar deck. On that steel deck, I could do nothing to save myself, but a strong hand reached out and caught my arm, it held me until I could get a grip on the elevator rail. I still don't know whom to thank for saving my life. Perhaps, the Lord himself.

I made my way to the high side. In the rolling water of the Pacific Ocean I saw nearly 2,000 heads bobbing in the sea, and I was going to join them. The deck crew topside had hung two-inch lines on the high side of the ship from the flight deck down to the water. Men from the bridge and flight deck descended on the lines down to the water. Men from below decks climbed up to the hangar deck and found a place on the lines to lower themselves into the water. With the port edge of our hanger touching the water, we had to go over the starboard high side to avoid being under the ship in case of capsizing.

Like all the others, I took off all my clothes down to my skivvies so as not to be weighted down. Someone threw me a Mae West life jacket, and I gratefully put it on.

It was then, in the midst of that serious struggle for life, I saw something that still makes me smile when I think back on it. Down below in the damaged ship, most of us had removed our wet shoes to climb the sloping decks and ladders, but topside the disciplined navy men had taken off their shoes and lined them up neatly on the hanger deck.

The crew had been taught and cautioned not to jump or dive into the water from the deck of the ship. There could be debris or other unseen objects under water that could injure or even kill them. However, some men did dive off.

I must stress again that in the bombing, the torpedo blasts, and even when it appeared the ship might capsize, I felt no fear. I am not necessarily a fearless type of person, but the miraculous had happened...God removed my fears the night I prayed in my bunk.

Determined to leave the ship and go down one of the lines into the sea, I moved closer to the upper edge of the hanger deck. All lines were filled, but eventually I found a place and grasped the two-inch line. I lowered myself down the side of the ship and into the waiting oil-covered water. Some men received terrible rope burns as they slid down the lines. Fortunately there were no sharks, for the explosions had scared them away.

Oil gushing from the fuel tanks had covered the water with several inches of thick ooze. The water was warm and oily, and we were about three miles from the nearest land, *straight down below us!* Oil got in our hair, our eyes, our noses, and our ears. We tried to keep it out of our mouths, though some failed to do so and became nauseous and vomited.

Our main and immediate concern was to get away from the ship in case it should capsize or go down and take us with it.

Saved by a Destroyer

The destroyers of Task Force 17 eased ever so slowly and carefully among groups of men to rescue us and take us aboard. These "Small Boys" hung cargo nets over the sides of their ships, but we could not swim in the oily water. We had no choice but to float and wait for the sea to wash us up against the side of one of the ships. Then, when we clung to the cargo nets, men on the ship were positioned to pull us on board.

Several times the ships pulled away from us because of more air raid alerts, so the operation lasted for hours. As the day wore on, motor whale boats (small personnel boats) from ships in the area towed lines behind them. Many of us were able to grasp the lines and were dragged to the ships and hauled aboard. This was the case when the boats were filled to capacity with men, and no more could get into them.

As I have said, it was in the oily water of the Pacific that my mind went home to my childhood and youth and to my beloved Verna. None of this seemed real, but reality was home and in my faith in God. The vastness of the sea, the previously unimaginable sight of our dying ship, and the whole enormity of the situation were beyond anything for which anyone could be prepared, and yet I knew my God was bigger than it all.

After hours in the water and with my strength almost gone, I found myself near the Destroyer BALCH. At last, the waves hurled me up against the side of the ship, and I grasped at the net for all my might. The net itself now posed a great problem and was most difficult for me, for my hands were greasy from the oil. Nearly exhausted from my ordeal of being exposed to the sea for several hours, I had little strength left. The sea had taken its toll, and I could hardly hold onto the nets. In one of the most difficult physical challenges of my life, I drew from some reserve of strength I had never known and raised myself up the net. Hands reached down to me, and I was pulled over the gunwale and onto the steel deck. Never has anything solid beneath me felt better than that hard metal deck!

A sailor was offering us cigarettes, but I replied, "I don't need that."

With brown oil on our faces and in our hair, it was difficult to recognize anyone; however, just after I got aboard the BALCH one of the men on the crowded deck recognized me and yelled, "There's 'the Deacon'! He was a member of the Bible group!"

Six or seven of us from the YORKTOWN Bible class were united at that moment, and others were picked up by other destroyers. Those of us on the BALCH turned in unison and made our way to the fan-tail (stern) of the ship, where barefooted and clad only in our skivvies we knelt on the steel deck and had an open-air praise meeting in full view of six or seven hundred sailors. With our oil-covered, weary hands raised in praise, we worshiped God openly and unashamed. We thanked Him for saving us in battle, for helping us escape the sinking ship, and for rescuing us from the sea. No one was embarrassed. As far as I know, only one man in our Bible study group was lost at the sinking of the YORKTOWN, and someday in heaven we will see him again. Surely, God was at Midway!

The crew of the destroyer BALCH treated us well. Men got into their personal lockers and gave clothing and candy to those of us who had nothing. A great spirit of camaraderie prevailed, for we were like a large family. In essence they were saying, "What's mine is yours."

There were not enough beds for all of us, so we had to "hot bunk" it. When members of the BALCH's crew got up from their bunks to go on watch, some of the rescued men went to bed in their bunks to catch a few winks.

That night, with hundreds of us on the open decks and overloading the small ship, the BALCH gunnery department decided to disarm its five-inch guns by "unloading through the muzzles." That is, they would fire the guns rather than take the ammunition out by hand. It is faster and easier.

Navy policy is to announce such an action, but they did not inform us they were going to do this. So when they fired, the explosions came unexpectedly. On the first crack of gunfire, we flinched and nearly jumped out of our skins and over the side. After a bit, we began to settle down and, with nervous laughter, began to joke about our predicament.

For us the Battle of Midway was over, but the YORKTOWN was yet to suffer its worst indignity.

Another Miracle at Midway

When some of the ships of our task force headed back to Pearl Harbor, the Destroyer HUGHES was ordered to stand by the derelict YORKTOWN to keep a watch on her.

When we had abandoned ship, two men, Seaman First Class George K. Weise from the Fourth Division and Norman M. Pichette of the Third Division, had been left in the sick bay to die. It was thought they could not live due to their wounds. In the bombing attack, Weise had received a skull fracture and was partially paralyzed, drifting in and out of consciousness; and Pichette had been severely wounded by shrapnel in the abdomen. Weise told this incredible story of their escape from the blackened compartment. (*Yorktown Crier,* 50th Anniversay Edition, June 4, 1992, pages 36-37)

"I was unconscious in the dressing room and during my trip to sick bay. I regained consciousness as the battle horn started blowing, along with the call to abandon ship. There were no lights, only the blue battle lanterns. The third class pharmacist's mate had his arm around me holding me up while asking the first class mate, 'What about him?' The first class mate said, 'Leave him, he's gonna die anyway.' The sailor who held me was crying during the entire ordeal because he didn't want to leave me.

"Consciousness would come and go, lasting only long enough for me to totally realize and understand my perilous situation. I thought I was hallucinating. Someone was calling my name again, and it was real. Norman Pichette, a seaman from the Third Division was calling me. He kept asking,'What can we do?' I told him to wrap a sheet around his waist and stomach and try to get on deck to fire a machine gun, and perhaps someone would know we were still on board.

"With a sheet tied around his wounded waist, Pichette got to his feet and made his way up the rickety ladders hanging from the slanting decks, from the third deck to topside. He found a machine gun and fired it into the water to get the attention of the crew of the HUGHES, which was standing by. The commanding officer of the HUGHES sent a boat over to YORKTOWN and got him. When he was taken aboard, he went unconscious on the deck; but after a few minutes Pichette regained consciousness for a few moments and mumbled that there was another man alive in the YORKTOWN. Norman Pichette died, having performed one of the great heroic acts of the war; the HUGHES sent a boat to rescue George Weise."

With Battle Flags Flying

The YORKTOWN did not sink that day. In fact, it looked as if she might not go down. Captain Buckmaster took a salvage crew back aboard to stabilize the ship and possibly tow it back to Pearl Harbor. The VIREO was sent out from Pearl Harbor to tow it.

At 6:15 a.m. on June 6, the YORKTOWN's salvage party went aboard to try to save the ship if at all possible. The plan was to put out fires and inspect the ship to ascertain the extent of the damage. Also, they wished to right the ship by off-loading removable weights such as guns or aircraft on the port side and counter-flooding. The rudder had been jammed, so they intended to free it for towing. The medical doctor and his group also went aboard to identify and collect the dead.

Meanwhile the Destroyer HAMMANN came alongside to provide electricity, hoses, and water to fight fires. However, on June 6, while this operation was in progress, the Japanese submarine I-168 found the crippled carrier with the HAMMANN alongside and from 1,200 yards fired four torpedoes. One hit the HAMMANN, sinking it within about five minutes with a great loss of life.

Two torpedoes hit the YORKTOWN below the bilge keels. Yet, the stubborn ship stayed afloat the night of June 6. On the morning of June 7, at 7:01 a.m., the YORKTOWN slowly turned over on her port side and gently let herself down into her watery grave. She disappeared into the sea as the murky water closed about her. She sank in about 3,000 fathoms (18,000 feet) of water, her battle flags still flying.

All hands who were topside on nearby ships stood at attention with heads uncovered, tears in their eyes. Ships half-masted their colors in salute to the brave ship. Two patrolling PBY's (large amphibious patrol bombers) appeared overhead and dipped their wings in a final salute.

Captain Buckmaster sent this message to the Secretary of the Navy:

> "I have to report that, as a result of damage sustained from three bomb hits and two torpedo hits received in action with the enemy on June 4, 1942, and two torpedo hits from enemy submarine attack on June 6, 1942, the U.S.S. YORKTOWN sank in LAT 30° 46' N: Long 167° 24' West, at 1701 (GCT) June 7, 1942."

In an even more dramatic statement, Captain Buckmaster sent the following message to the Commander of Task Force 17, Admiral Jack Frank Fletcher, USN:

"As dawn broke on June 7, 1942, the YORKTOWN was observed to have increased her list to port; her flight deck touched the water. It was apparent that she would sink. At 0645 all ships half-masted colors; at 0700:30 ATTENTION was ordered, all hands uncovered; and at 0701 the U.S.S. YORKTOWN (CV-5) sank in LAT 30º 46' N., Longitude 167º 24' W."

He signed it, "Captain Buckmaster."

It was over. The Battle of Midway had been fought and won against all odds. It was the end of serious Japanese expansion. Shortly thereafter, the American forces began to drive back the would-be conquerors. U.S. Marines attacked the Solomon Islands in August, and a month later American and Australian forces began to drive the Japanese out of New Guinea. The Battle of Midway was the turning point of the war.

I am sometimes asked what happened to the planes from the YORKTOWN. The truth is we lost most of our aircraft at Midway. The remaining planes not able to land on carriers were ditched at sea. The American fleet had lost the Aircraft Carrier YORKTOWN, the Destroyer HAMMANN, and 150 planes, while the Japanese had lost four aircraft carriers, two heavy cruisers, three destroyers, and 275 planes.

Thomas B. Allen wrote, "In the 44 months of fighting that followed [the attack on Pearl Harbor], the United States Navy sank every one of the Japanese aircraft carriers, battleships, and cruisers of the Pearl Harbor strike force." *(National Geographic* December 1991, page 75)

The USS YORKTOWN (CV-5) sank exactly six months to the day after the bombing of Pearl Harbor.

From December 7, 1941, 1942 listed were the following engagements in her wartines career of 182 days.

MARSHALL and
      GILBERT ISLANDS...............31 January, 1942
SALAMAUA and LAE.....................10 March, 1942
TULAGI (three attacks)..........................4 May, 1942
MISIMA ISLAND (sunk enemy carrier)......7 May, 1942
NIGHT ACTION (enemy planes)...............7 May, 1942
BATTLE of the CORAL SEA...................8 May, 1942
BATTLE of MIDWAY ISLAND...............4 June, 1942

Sailor-musician Stanford E. Linzey, Jr., clarinetist in the ship's band-
USS Yorktown (CV-5). Verna May Linzey took Stan to church on
their first date.

The 19,900 ton aircraft carrier USS YORKTOWN (CV-5) rides at anchor in San Diego (CA) Harbor in 1940. Mrs. Eleanor Roosevelt broke the bottle of champagne across her bow and said, "I christen thee Yorktown," after the famous revolutionary battle of Yorktown, VA   —US Navy Photo

US Marines guard "The last steak in captivity." USS YORTOWN had been at sea for 104 days, supplies and provisions were running low. The Chaplain held a jamboree on the flight deck and auctioned off this last steak. The band marched and played Sousa's marches-Tonga 1942.   —Photo courtesy of Bill and Mary Carpenter, Fresno, CA.

Captain Stanford E. Linzey, Jr., Chaplain Corps, U.S. Navy.
Command Chaplain in the aircraft carrier, USS CORAL
SEA (CVA–43), named after the famous Battle of the Coral
Sea.

Abandon ship! USS YORKTOWN (CV–5) received three direct bomb hits and two torpedoes from Japanese aircraft in The Battle of Midway, June 4, 1942. The ship took a list of 27° to the port side. Captain Elliott Buckmaster feared the ship might capsize ordered, "All hands, abandon ship!" —Official U.S. Navy Photo

PSALM 91:1-2,5-7

He that dwelleth in the secret place of the most High
shall abide under the shadow of the Almighty.
I will say of the Lord, He is my refuge and my fortress:
My God; in him will I trust.
Thou shalt not be afraid for the terror by night;
Nor for the arrow that flieth by day;
Nor for the pestilence that walketh in darkness;
Nor for the destruction that wasteth at noonday.
A thousand shall fall at thy side,
And ten thousand at thy right hand;
but it shall not come nigh thee.

Chapter Eight

Fruit of My Labors

The destroyer BALCH rescued over 500 YORKTOWN refugees from the sea. We were a motley-looking group of stragglers, barefooted, clad only in our underwear, and pathetically covered with brown oil. The thick goo of the oil slick was in our hair, eyes, ears, and noses. We were a pitiful sight, but we were alive!

The Battle in Retrospect

The ancient Israelites called their God the Lord of Hosts because of His deliverance in battle; and I, too, had a new relationship with Him in battle as the One who delivered me from death and from the awful fear that first had gripped me. When I think back to those moments when I lay in that third-deck compartment at about water level and waited for the torpedoes to strike, I realize but for the grace of God one of those Japanese torpedoes could have sent me down with the ship. I do not know why some men died and others survived; I only know God had a purpose for my life that was not yet fulfilled, and for that I praise His holy name and commit my life totally to His command.

The Destroyers MORRIS, HAMMANN, HUGHES, BENHAM, ANDERSON and RUSSELL picked up the rest of the survivors, about 2,200 in all.

The greatest naval battle ever staged, up to that time, had been fought and won; the greatest naval tonnage ever assembled for one encounter had been sunk or dispersed; and the greatest naval force ever to sail had been defeated by a numerically smaller force, that of the U.S. Navy.

The war in the Pacific ended in 1945 with the nuclear bombing of Hiroshima and Nagasaki, but the eventual outcome of the war was determined at Midway. Although fierce battles would be fought over different island groups, the United States had established the air and sea superiority that would be Japan's downfall. Today people may question why so much was fought over such tiny bits of land scattered across such a vast ocean, but Japan had intended those outposts only as part of a greater expansion into Hawaii, the Philippines, New Guinea, Australia, and Indonesia—in addition to its conquests of China, Korea, Vietnam, and Malaysia on the Asian mainland. The Battle of the Coral Sea stopped the southern advance of the Japanese, and the Battle of Midway turned the tide of the war.

A major player in both of those strategic battles was the USS YORKTOWN (CV-5), which rests proudly and peacefully below the rolling surface of the Pacific Ocean. She did what she was called upon to do, and as she went down with battle flags still flying she brought glory to the United States of America and honor to her proud survivors.

And then, in my moments of less glorious contemplation, I remember that somewhere down there still put away neatly in its case is my clarinet.

Hawaii Bound Again

With the YORKTOWN sunk, the survivors were steaming back on various ships to Pearl Harbor, Hawaii, for reassignment to other ships or shore stations. On the night of June 4, 1942, we sailors aboard the BALCH crowded the decks, some propped up against the bulkheads, many stretched out on the steel decks, and others sleeping up along the rail. Most of us kept a tin coffee cup on our belts and made frequent trips to the galley for refills. We drank coffee around the clock. It was a great source of pleasure.

None of us wished to go below decks, we were still in enemy waters and the memories of our escape from the YORKTOWN were very fresh on our minds. Danger lurked in the air above us and peril in the depths of the sea beneath us. We felt it best to be topside in any eventuality.

On the morning of June 5 we were transferred to the USS PORTLAND, a heavy cruiser with 8-inch guns and a compliment of a thousand officers and enlisted men. This ship had the space and capability to take care of us fairly adequately and comfortably, though we still were a little crowded. Aboard the PORTLAND we could eat and take showers regularly and had room to stretch out.

We made the transfer from BALCH to PORTLAND by highline. This is a normal ship-to-ship operation practiced by the Navy at sea. In this operation, a line is stretched from one ship to the other as the two ships steam side by side in close formation. A Bos'n's Chair hangs suspended from the line and rides on a wheel on the line.

A team of sailors on the deck force on each ship pull the chair back and forth on the line across the water from ship to ship with its passengers and let them off. This chair is pulled across time and again until all passengers are hauled across. All passengers in the chair are required to wear life vests, and a destroyer lags behind the formation to pick up anyone who should fall into the sea between the ships. It is a painstaking and dangerous operation, for ships can collide at sea or pull apart and snap the line.

Many years later, Commander John Stull, the executive officer of the SOUTHERLAND, played a trick on me when I was the chaplain to Destroyer Squadron 5, and temporarily berthed in his ship.

One Sunday, while I was in the process of transferring from the SOUTHERLAND to another ship to conduct Divine Services, he escorted me up to the deck and began to advise me of the risks involved. It was my first trip on the highline since my 1942 experience of boarding the PORTLAND, and he could see that I was having some apprehension about the operation.

Commander Stull always enjoyed a good joke and was a teaser. He was a large man and had his own personal life jacket, which fit him. It was large, new, and unsoiled with long straps to fit around him.

"Chaplain," he said, "this might be pretty dangerous for you on the line. I have a new life jacket and I'll send the messenger down to my stateroom to get it. You can wear it. It is new, and if you should fall into the drink it will take care of you."

I put it on, and it was very large. The straps wrapped around me a couple of times as I was submerged in it.

He continued as he observed my reactions. "Now, when you are riding the chair, if the ships lean inboard (toward each other), the lines will go limp and you will go into the water. But, stay with the chair. When the ships right themselves it will pull you out of the water, and the men will pull you across."

Then he said, "Now, if you hear a loud snap of the line, that means the ships have leaned outboard (apart from each other) and the line has parted. Then you will drop into the drink. In that case, get rid of the chair. If the ships do not pull you through the screws (propellers), the HENDERSON will be back there to pick you up when you get to it."

I sensed his prank and anticipation for some fun out of me as he waited for my reaction. "Thanks a lot, John. Thanks a lot." We both had a good laugh, and the transfer went off without a hitch.

This is a manner of transfer at sea performed by the Navy from ship to ship from time immemorial. Of course, now helicopters play a greater part in these transfers from ship to ship.

Another Bible Study

After I had gotten on board the PORTLAND on Friday, June 5, I remembered the Christian sailor to whom I had given the Gideon New Testaments a month earlier, after the Battle of the Coral Sea. He had come aboard YORKTOWN with the damage control party to study our damage control procedures. He was the lad with the Gideon New Testament in his uniform pocket and had been a Christian for only for a week. I had urged him to start a Bible class in his ship.

I looked him up. After a few words of greeting, I asked, "Have you started a Bible class in the ship?"

He looked at me a little downcast and replied, "No. I'm the only Christian in the ship."

"That can't be," I protested. "There are a thousand men in the ship. The odds are greater than a thousand to one that there are more Christians aboard than you alone."

We knew some of the men from the YORKTOWN's Bible class were on board, so I got the group together with this young man and announced," Tonight, we shall have a meeting forward on the fo'c'sle deck under the eight-inch guns at 7:00.p.m. Let's get the word out and invite men to come."

I got the officer of the deck to pass the word over the ship's speaker system announcing the meeting, and that night twenty–one men were in attendance. We sat on the deck and sang and prayed under the silent guns as the fo'c'sle deck heaved and fell in the surging sea.

It was about dusk when we began but still light enough to read the Scriptures, which would be followed by testimonies, singing, and prayers. Although we had no hymnals, we sang mostly the old hymns that the men from the denominational churches knew, at least those we could remember. We had no hymnals. Afterwards I brought a short message of encouragement to the men.

At the conclusion of the meeting, I urged the group, "If we are still onboard tomorrow night we shall meet again, same time, same place. Let's get the word out and be here."

We never knew from one day to the next where we would be, or whether we would be transferred, but on Saturday night, June 6th, thirty–two men gathered for devotions, prayer, singing, and testimonies.

When I asked if someone would like to testify, one sailor spoke up and began to weep as he spoke. I thought something had happened to upset him. Maybe bad news from home. In tears he said, "I have been on this ship for over two years, and I didn't know there was another Christian in the ship but me."

Of the thirty–two men present, I found that five of them belonged to the PORTLAND's ship's company. That is, they were members of that crew. They did not know each other and accordingly did not know the others were Christians. No one was talking.

We had a spiritual meeting, and all hands were blessed and encouraged.

It is impossible in a large ship to know everybody. For example, on one occasion in the USS AMERICA, a large aircraft carrier with over 5,000 men aboard, one man went AWOL (absent without leave) while in the ship. He never left the ship at any time but was simply absent without leave from his appointed place of duty. No one could locate him.

When a man lives in one end of a large ship, often he does not know the men in the other end of the vessel. The man in the carrier had left his berthing space and gone to another area of the ship, and those people thought he was a new man on board. No one thought to question him. They finally caught him when he got in line to be paid.

After our meeting that night, I got the five PORTLAND men together and spoke with them until about midnight. I encouraged them to get themselves together, organize a Bible class, be regular and faithful in attendance, and be a witness for Jesus Christ throughout the ship. I reminded them there were other believers in the ship who would rally around them once they started.

I was only an enlisted sailor then, yet looking back on those days, I have realized God's calling on my life to be a chaplain was quite apart from any later appointment. God had already anointed me to do the ministry my church and the Navy would later recognize and endorse.

I felt the apostle Paul and I had something in common. I certainly would not place myself on his spiritual level, but we did share in one common event, *"I suffered shipwreck and have been in the deep."* (**2 Corinthians 11:25)** God was good to both of us in rescuing and saving us. He had work for us to do.

Days at Pearl Harbor

On Sunday morning, June 7, we were transferred to the FULTON, at that time the Navy's newest submarine tender. FULTON had been sent out by Admiral Nimitz to ake the YORKTOWN crew to Pearl Harbor. FULTONt received on board that day 101 officers and 1,790 enlisted men for atotal of 1,891 seamen, 59 of whom were stretcher cases. We arrived in Hawaii on June 8. Some of the YORKTOWN men were still on other ships. They were dispersed throughout the fleet for transportation back to Pearl Harbor.

When we sailed into Pearl Harbor, Admiral Nimitz met us. The crew was immediately taken to Camp Catlin, a Marine base on the Island of Oahu, where we stayed until reassignment to other ships or shore stations.

We were broke and penniless. We could not be paid, for our pay records had gone down with the ship. We had no liberty, for we had no uniforms nor civilian clothing. All we had were the dungarees on our backs. The American Red Cross lent us money and gave us health and comfort items such as toilet articles until we were paid. Finally, we did get paid and were outfitted in uniforms.

Not only this, but the command did not let us out in town for fear we would tell of the sinking of the YORKTOWN. It was still top secret that we had lost the aircraft carrier.

Yet Another Bible Study

One day, I went over to the receiving barracks in Pearl Harbor to check on my records. I discovered a group of enlisted men were meeting for Bible study in an air raid shelter behind the barracks. Always interested in witnessing, fellowship, and spreading the gospel, I attended one of the meetings.

I asked the group leader, "Do you people have permission to meet here in the shelter? Does the command know you are here?" I knew that the Navy had always taken a dim view of personnel meeting in secret chambers for fear of clandestine motives.

The petty officer replied that they did not have permission nor authority to meet and did not know whether the command knew.

"Why not?" I asked. "Get proper authority or you may get in trouble and cause yourselves difficulty with the command."

"Will you get permission for us?" the petty officer asked. I affirmed I would.

The following day, I went to see the 14th Naval District chaplain, Commander Thornton Miller, USN. I said I was off the YORKTOWN and told him of the meeting in the air raid shelter. We wanted him to be aware of it, and we wanted his permission to continue. I told him the times of meeting, how we conducted our services, and everything else about it. I even said we would be happy to have him join us when he could.

The chaplain said, "That's fine. Keep up the good work." I thanked him, and as I started for the door he asked, "By the way, Linzey, what church do you belong to?"

"The Assemblies of God," I replied.

"Well, that's fine," he said. "We just have to be careful. We don't want any holy rollers down there."

"Don't worry about that, Chaplain," I responded. "We've got it under control." I had to smile to myself as I left his office.

Chaplain Thornton Miller became a close personal friend to me. He was eventually promoted to the rank of Rear Admiral in the Chaplain Corps, U.S. Navy. Many years later he made it possible and was responsible for me to re-enter the Navy as a chaplain.

Treasure Island

In July, 1942, I departed Pearl Harbor and set sail in the HENDERSON for San Francisco and Treasure Island for reassignment. The HENDERSON was an old transport ship and perhaps the slowest vessel in the Navy. It could sail at only eight knots per hour. If she had met up with an enemy submarine, she would probably take a direct hit and sink almost immediately. She was an open ship with very little water-tight integrity.

We refugees from YORKTOWN and Midway stayed topside during most of the voyage from Hawaii to San Francisco. We did not want to take any chances at this time, having escaped the Battles of the Coral Sea and Midway, we did not want to be caught again below deck. Our good fortune might have run out. As on the other ships since Midway, we kept tin cups on our belts and drank coffee around the clock. Besides eating, this was the only pleasure we had on board. There was nothing else to do but wait until we arrived in California.

After eight days at sea, we arrived in San Francisco and sailed under the Golden Gate Bridge. To us, this was a beautiful sight. We were home from the war. We were taken to the Treasure Island Naval Station in the middle of the San Francisco Bay to await further transfer. San Francisco was to the west and Oakland to the east. The skylines in the summer of 1942 were quite different than those of today. Treasure Island was partially created with stone, mud and clay from the making of the tunnels on Yerba Buena Island for the 1939 World's Fair. After the Fair, the man-made island was used by the Navy.

While waiting for our orders on Treasure Island, we were given leave. Verna had come up to San Francisco and was staying with me in the Keystone Hotel, so we took leave and went home to San Diego. We rode Southern Pacific Railroad's "Daylight Special" down through Los Angeles and home.

Verna's mother told her that if we could stop in Los Angeles and visit Reverend. and Mrs. Harms, "Stan may receive the baptism in the Holy Spirit."

The Rev. Raymond Harms, a personal friend of Verna's parents, was an official of the California Evangelistic Association and pastor of the church. Rev. F.L. Doyle, Verna's stepfather, had encouraged Raymond Harms to enter the ministry many years before when he was a young man in Missouri.

We visited the Harmses and went to a prayer meeting in their church one evening. The next morning, we were in prayer again when I received a wonderful infilling of the Holy Spirit and spoke in my spiritual prayer language as the first Christians did on the Day of Pentecost. God had answered Verna's prayers for me.

Ministry in Florida

I prayed that the Lord would give our band shore duty. If we did not have to go back to sea again while the war was still on, I promised I would be faithful in giving my time to conduct a Bible study on the base where I was stationed.

Our orders came, and our band was transferred to Miami, Florida, to form the 7th Naval District Band. Wonderful! We knew we were going to be ashore for a while.

The Navy had taken over the hotels in Miami to be used for office space and dormitories. The band was stationed in the Everglades Hotel and later moved over to the Dolphin Hotel, where we remained.

In Miami, I began to preach in earnest and hold Bible classes in the hotels. In the Everglades Hotel the Lord reminded me of my promise, so I organized a group meeting on the 17th floor of the hotel. We met one night each week.

On the first night of meeting, as I got on the elevator to go up to the meeting room, another sailor got on with me. We introduced ourselves; he was Soundman Second Class Morris R. Barrons from Michigan. He was an enthusiastic young Christian sailor. He told me about himself and his church and inquired of my religious status. I said, "I use to belong to your church." He looked very hurt and asked, "Don't you still believe?"

I replied that I did but that in addition to that I had received the baptism in the Holy Spirit. He said, "My wife and I read Acts 2:4 in the Bible last night and wondered what it meant." I explained it to him and both he and his wife received the Holy Spirit and became ministers in the group.

When Morris got out of the Navy, he attended Southwestern Bible College in Waxahachie, Texas. He went to Rome, Texas, and organized and built the Assemblies of God church there in 1948. While in Rome, he became close friends with the young Methodist pastor. In his first Pentecostal revival in Rome in 1950, the Methodist pastor received a wonderful infilling of the Spirit. That man, Pastor Johnnie Barnes, eventually resigned his church and became an itinerant evangelist for a short while and later pastored the Assembly of God in Electra, Texas. In fact, I invited him to conduct a revival for me in El Cajon, California, with great success.

In the course of time, Johnnie Barnes founded a program for boys he called Royal Rangers, which became the national boys' ministry of the Assemblies of God. Royal Rangers has had a far-reaching effect on the youth of the church and now is a worldwide movement with leaders in many nations. Besides its scouting-type and religious training and camping for the boys, the program has given opportunities for ministry to many thousands of men.

Johnnie Barnes became the national commander of the Royal Rangers program until his untimely death.

Over the years God continued to bless my efforts. The God who had been with me at Midway was also the God of the Everglades Hotel. I had kept my promises to Him, and He had kept His.

I taught Sunday school classes in Evangel Temple with Dr. C.O. Neece, the pastor, and held street meetings with the youth in the park in Miami Beach. In September, 1943, I was licensed to preach for the Assemblies of God. I was a sailor not yet 23 years old, but now I was a preacher.

While in Florida, I accepted the pastorate of a small church in the city of Goulds, about 23 miles south of Miami. I served this church with success for about six months until I was transferred again.

One Saturday night, I went out onto Flagler Street in downtown Miami in uniform and began to hand out gospel tracts. This was in 1944, and the war was still on. So, there were many servicemen on the streets as well as civilians. The Navy Shore Patrol swung by in their jeep and picked me up. The driver said, "Get in, Sailor," and they took me down to the Shore Patrol station and had me arraigned before the officer in charge.

"What's the charge, Officer," I asked. He looked over the tracts for some time and finally replied, "Well, you are not supposed to be handing out this material on the streets."

"Yes, but what is the charge?" I pressed.

"Well, you are not supposed to do this." I kept pressing for a reason for picking me and hauling me down to the Shore Patrol office as if I were some criminal. The Shore Patrol's job was to handle miscreant sailors in navy towns when they cause trouble. Finally, he let me go with the warning I was not to stand on the streets and hand out tracts.

The following week I went to visit the 7th Naval District chaplain, Captain C.V. Ellis, USN, and told him what had happened.

Chaplain Ellis was a fine Baptist chaplain, an older man, having served for many years in the Navy. He was a man of grace and charm. He had taken an interest in me, for he knew I had aspirations about the ministry. He was wise in counsel with good advice to a young navy man. He enjoyed it, too.

When I told him the Shore Patrol had picked me up and hauled me in the previous week for handing out tracts, the chaplain became upset over it. He questioned me about it and then picked up the phone and called the Shore Patrol headquarters. He raised havoc with the Shore Patrol officer for his actions and wound up by warning him that he, the chaplain, did not want to hear again that the Shore Patrol had picked up a sailor on the streets of Miami for handing out gospel literature.

That ended that story!

I used to visit Chaplain Ellis often for counsel and advice, and he was gracious to receive me and talk. One day I told him I was planning to leave the Navy and become a preacher.

He tested me about my call. "How do you know you are called to preach?" he asked.

I thought about it for a few moments and replied, "Well, Chaplain, I like to preach and I have a desire to preach. I like to study the Bible, and I have seen some success in my ministry."

The old chaplain softly replied, "Well, that's how you know."

I decided the ministry was for me and began to prepare myself for it. I took correspondence courses prepared by the church. I was receiving my practical ministry under the direction of Dr. Neece and through my pastorate in Goulds.

But yet, I loved navy life and wished to stay in the Navy for a career. I felt I could accomplish much more for the Lord as a navy chaplain than I could as an enlisted man. So, I set my sights on that goal. In this manner, I could fulfil my call to the ministry and perform these duties in the Navy. I could have the best of both worlds.

The war in the Pacific was still on. In November, 1942, I heard that the Cruiser PORTLAND had been sunk in the Battle of Guadalcanal. This proved to be incorrect, although the ship had been torpedoed by the Japanese in Iron Bottom Sound—the body of water between Florida Island and Guadalcanal in the Solomon Islands. It was so named because so many ships—Japanese and American—were sunk there.

I was discouraged when I learned of the PORTLAND's misfortune, for I had given part of my life in trying to help the men of that ship find Christ and had established a Bible class in the ship for the furtherance of the gospel.

Surely, I had no right to be disheartened, for it is God's work, after all. But, I was upset. I felt I would never know how the group fared or succeeded. I would never get feedback on my efforts. I had hoped to hear of the good that might have come from those classes.

New Assignments

From Miami, I went back to the Navy School of Music in Washington, D.C., for reassignment. I was privileged to go as first clarinetist and assistant bandmaster with a new band for assignment to the Kaneohe Naval Air Station, Oahu, Hawaii. The band was under the direction of Chief Musician John A. Liegl, who had been my clarinet instructor in the School of Music. He was a genteel Austrian gentleman and a fine clarinetist. I was honored to work with him.

On several occasions, at Kaneohe Naval Air Station, I spoke to John about Jesus Christ, seemingly with no results. When I returned to San Diego for reassignment, I awaited orders at Camp Elliot. I was attached to the band on the station directed by Chief Musician Saucier.

One morning when I reported in to the station, to my surprise I met Bandmaster Liegl. He had just returned from Hawaii for reassignment. We had a good reunion.

Verna and I invited Liegl out to our church, First Assembly of God in San Diego. We had a fine service on a Sunday night, and when the invitation was given John leaned over and said to me, "What do they mean by getting saved?"

I briefly explained the message to him and, at his insistence, I accompanied the bandmaster to the altar where he gave his heart to Jesus Christ.

To my dismay, the Navy closed Camp Elliot, and I had to leave home again. I was sent back to the School of Music in Washington, D.C., for reassignment and was ordered to San Juan, Puerto Rico, for assignment in the band at the Naval Air Station. I served in this band for about six months. Then I was released from the Navy after serving as an enlisted musician for a period of eight years, one month and 14 days.

Destination Chaplaincy

I returned to Jacksonville, Florida, and was separated from the Naval Service in February, 1947. Then I took the train westward to San Diego, my wife, children, and home. There I entered the Linda Vista Baptist Bible College and Seminary under the presidency of Dr. Otto Reese, to begin my theological training. The naval chaplaincy was my goal.

While pursuing my education, at 26 years of age, I set out to organize and build a church in the city of El Cajon. The church we called the Evangelistic Tabernacle was later renamed the New Life Family Center.

In the Sunday evening services, after the hymn singing, we always had testimony time. The folks could tell the group how God had answered prayer or met their needs in some particular way. It was encouraging and therapeutic.

One Sunday night, Peggy Givens and her husband Sam— total strangers to our congregation—attended the evening service. During the testimony service she stood to her feet and asked, "May I testify?"

I replied that she might, and she told this amazing story:

"My son was a sailor in the Cruiser PORTLAND during the Battle of Guadalcanal in 1942. The ship was torpedoed in the battle, and my son was killed in the action. But, before the battle someone in the ship had witnessed to him about Jesus Christ, and he gave his heart to the Lord. I'm going to see my son in heaven."

Harry O'Neal Fitzsimmons was a young seaman in the USS PORTLAND sailing with Admiral Callaghan's task force of five cruisers and eight destroyers in the Solomon Islands when they met and engaged the Japanese fleet about 1:30 in the morning of Friday, November 12, 1942. The Battle of Guadalcanal was fought in the dark.

The PORTLAND took an aerial torpedo "up the skirts," that is, in the stern. The rudder jammed and she went in circles. Young Fitzsimmons was one of eighteen men who were killed in the ship that night.

Neal Fitzsimmons was a twenty-one-year-old sailor from Potosi, Missouri. Previous to his joining the Navy he had worked in the hospital unit in the Civilian Conservation Corps (CCC). He had joined the Navy to become a medical corpsman with the hopes of eventually becoming a doctor.

Neal was working in the laundry aboard the PORTLAND awaiting an opening in the medical ranks. He has been stationed in the bow section of the ship, but just two days before the battle he was transferred to the stern section and and was killed there in the torpedo attack.

Many years later, I met Neal's brother Gary, a veteran Navy chief petty officer, in Bakersfield, California. He had served in the Navy during the war. As we spoke of Neal, Gary reminisced philosophically, "I believe I can see the wisdom of the good Lord in taking Neal when He did. It's easier to serve the Lord in a ship than on shore where many temptations confront the sailor. Perhaps the good Lord in His wisdom felt Neal might not have stood the test of living for Him. We both had been 'party boys' before becoming Christians. Neal may never have gotten saved otherwise."

Neal Fitzsimmons was awarded the Purple Heart posthumously for giving his life for his country. I am so grateful to God that I had a part in getting the gospel to him.

Gary was the last family member to see Neal alive. Gary's ship, the USS PERKINS, had gone alongside the PORTLAND out in the middle of the vast Pacific Ocean to refuel. Neal came to the stern of the PORTLAND and Gary on the stern of the PERKINS, and they talked to each other—actually they had to yell—for over an hour from ship to ship as they traveled on parallel course in close formation while the PORTLAND transferred fuel to the PERKINS. This was on May 5, 1942.

"I got word of Neal's death while I was in the Aleutian Islands many weeks after the event," Gary said. "Mail came aboard late one night, and I was informed of my brother's death. He was killed on Friday, November 12, 1942."

Gary's and Neal's mother, Mrs. Peggy Givens, was the granddaughter of a Baptist minister. However, she had not made a profession of faith until the attack on Pearl Harbor. Having two sons in the Navy, she had immediately become concerned for their safety. She attended the Assemblies of God Church in San Ysidro, California, (Rev. Paul Ballard, pastor) and committed her life to

Christ and His church. She practiced her faith diligently until the time of her death. She passed away in a rest home in Yuma, Arizona, at the age of 96. Verna and I had the privilege of visiting her before her death. When she recognized us, she spoke aloud, "Praise God! Praise God!"

Gary Fitzsimmons said, "Mother prayed for us boys ten to fifteen times a day. I accepted the Lord on the Mount of Olives in the Intercontinental Hotel. We were on a Holy Land tour led by the Reverend Ralph Harris. That was in 1976. Mother prayed until her four children and her husband had accepted the Lord Jesus Christ. Mother's prayers for her boys were answered."

What a story! I could hardly believe my ears. I had heard from God. My efforts in the Pacific during those war years had not been in vain. This was the feedback I needed and which gave me great encouragement. I know I shall see at least one man in heaven due to my efforts in the PORTLAND in those weary days of battle at sea. Perhaps, I'll see many more.

Through it all, I realized that God was at Midway.

Chapter Nine

For God
and Country

During my years as an enlisted sailor, I had felt an increasing sense of divine calling to be a U.S. Navy chaplain. On the YORKTOWN, I had conducted Bible studies and was known as "the Deacon". In fact, with the exception of being on a sinking ship or floating in an oil slick in the Pacific Ocean, I loved navy life and could see myself in a navy career. I had completed the Berean College course, been licensed to preach with the Assemblies of God in the Peninsular Florida District, and was later ordained to the ministry in the Southern California District. I decided to continue my education and work toward the chaplaincy while pastoring churches.

I built and pastored the Evangelistic Tabernacle in El Cajon, California, for seven and a half years, during which time it grew to be one of the leading churches in the area. The city of El Cajon is about fifteen miles east of San Diego.

When I was a twenty-six-year-old minister, I stood on Mt. Helix, which looks over El Cajon Valley, and asked God to give me the valley and to help me build a church that would be a landmark in the area. He did just that.

Pastoring a church was a fulltime job in itself but, at the same time, I enrolled in the Linda Vista Baptist Bible College and Seminary on the G.I. Bill. This helped me financially, as I had the care of a wife and our first four children. On top of this load, I took a job as custodian at Standard Brands Foods in San Diego (at $1.00 per hour) to help put bread on the table. I really, had my hands full.

Busy as I was with pastoring and caring for my family, I laid out of school three times and was tempted to quit. I got so tired, but Dr. Eddie Sivertsen, the academic dean, persuaded me to hang in and continue my education. For that, I shall always appreciate him.

Meanwhile, I kept in touch with Admiral Thornton Miller, the chaplain for the 11th Naval District, who coached me along with his encouragement and gave me a recommendation for entrance into the Navy Chaplain Corps. He put me across.

Verna was and is a good, faithful wife, who kept the children quiet so "daddy could study". This went on for seven and one-half years and other children. Verna and I have ten children, all of whom have made us very, very proud.

In the summer of 1954, we moved to Baldwin Park, California, where I pastored the First Assembly of God. I finished my seminary education in the California Baptist Theological Seminary in Covina, California, taking my Master of Divinity degree. This seminary merged and is now the American Baptist Seminary of the West in Berkeley, California. Many years later after my retirement from the Navy, I went on in 1980 to receive my doctorate in Theology at Fuller Theological Seminary in Pasadena, California.

My Career as Chaplain

Upon graduation from seminary, I made application to the Navy Chaplain Corps, was accepted, and went on active duty on July 1, 1955, with the rank of lieutenant-junior grade (LTJG). I served the Navy as a chaplain on many different assignments for another twenty years, rising through the officer ranks and eventually attaining the rank of captain. I was the first Assemblies of God minister to serve as a chaplain in the regular officer corps of the U.S. Navy and, upon attaining the rank of captain, became the highest-ranking naval officer in the Assemblies of God at that time.

My last tour of sea duty was that of Command Chaplain in the Aircraft Carrier USS CORAL SEA (CVA-43), named after the famous battle in which I had participated years before. What a difference it was to be an officer in the CORAL SEA compared to being a seaman in the YORKTOWN! Each of those great aircraft carriers was at the cutting edge of technology in its day, and I was proud to serve my Lord on both of them.

History will have forgotten that the CORAL SEA became known as "the Pentecostal ship" because more than one hundred officers and seamen were baptized in the Holy Spirit and spoke in their spiritual prayer language during my tour of service. We had a weekly charismatic service in addition to the Protestant Divine Services and noonday devotions. With the exception of two men, all who were in the noonday devotions received the baptism in the Holy Spirit. Of those who later went out of the Navy, twenty-eight to thirty became pastors or evangelists in various Evangelical and Pentecostal churches. Four became Pentecostal military chaplains, and one is a bible college President.

While in active service, I spoke by invitation during the Pentagon Prayer Breakfast on the subject of the baptism in the Holy Spirit. Several received the baptism in the Holy Spirit on that occasion. I later reported this event in my first book, *Pentecost in the Pentagon,* (Exposition Press, 1975).

A Holy Spirit Ministry

After two decades as a chaplain, I retired from the U.S. Navy in 1974 and, for the next year, served as pastor of an Assemblies of God congregation in Vista, California. Then, due to my experience in teaching on the Holy Spirit and leading people into a personal experience of the baptism in the Holy Spirit, and what I felt to be the calling of God, I left the pastorate to begin holding seminars and preaching in churches on the ministry and work of the Spirit. In addition to holding Holy Spirit Seminars for the churches and speaking for the Full Gospel and Business Men's Fellowship USA. I have lectured at Indiana University in Bloomington, Indiana, at Seattle Pacific University, California State University at Fullerton, and the University of the Ryukyus in Okinawa, Japan. I have long since lost count of the thousands of believers who have been baptized in the Holy Spirit under my ministry. For this, I gratefully praise the Lord, who spared my life for His own purpose.

Over the twenty years of this evangelistic ministry, my faithful wife Verna has been my constant companion. How many miles we have driven! How many motel rooms we have occupied! How many church services we have enjoyed together!

I have often been asked about this ministry of leading people into the baptism in the Holy Spirit. This experience of being filled with the Holy Spirit and speaking in other tongues is a distinctive feature of all Pentecostal and charismatic churches whose doctrine is based upon the foundation of original, New Testament Christianity. In the early church, all Christian believers were expected to receive this experience. On the Day of Pentecost, *"They were all filled with the Holy Ghost, and began to speak with other tongues, as the Spirit gave them utterance."* **(Acts 2:4).** On that same day, Peter said, *"Repent, and be baptized every one of you...and ye shall receive the gift of the Holy Ghost."* **(Acts 2:38).** *The apostle Paul said, "I would that ye all spake with tongues."* **(1 Corinthians 14:5)**

I have found when people are taught the value of New Testament Christianity they tend to receive the New Testament experiences of personal salvation, the baptism in the Holy Spirit, and such miraculous events as divine-healing and the leading of the Spirit.

In most church services where I preach, I give a biblical explanation of the Holy Spirit baptism and then invite people to come forward to receive what Jesus called, *"the promise of the Father"*. **(Acts 1:4)** With the pastor, I go down the line and pray with each one, many of them are filled with the Holy Spirit and speak in other tongues. Over the years, many of these people have gone on in the power of the Spirit to do exploits for God.

One such example was Teresa Tamura, a Japanese member of Twin Palms Assembly of God in San Jose, California (David Womack, pastor). An author of books that explain American law to Japanese businessmen and the writer of widely distributed newspaper columns, she is well known in the Japanese American community. When we prayed with her, she began to speak in a language that was neither English nor Japanese. Within a few months, as an outreach of that church she and her husband Al, who had been confined to American prison camps during World War II, started a fifteen-minute gospel program in Japanese that came on right after the Japanese news on San Francisco's Channel 26. Between her television ministry, her home Bible studies, and her newspaper writing she has proclaimed the gospel of Jesus Christ to nearly every Japanese–speaking person in the United States.

Jesus said, *"But ye shall receive power, after that the Holy Ghost is come upon you: and ye shall be witnesses unto me."* **(Acts 1:8)** I could tell of hundreds of others who have gone on to be witnesses of the gospel to many people. I know now that it was for this cause the Lord proved His power to me at the Battle of Midway and called me to this ministry.

Our Pride and Joy

Verna and I thank God for the influence we have had on many people over the years, but our greatest joy is in the accomplishments of our ten children. Four of the five boys are ministers, four of the five girls are married to ministers, David is principal of a middle school, in Chino, California. Eugene is an operations officer in a nuclear laboratory, in Los Alamos, New Mexico; Janice is the executive assistant to the city administrator, in the city of Pomona, California; Sharon is a professor at Pacific Christian College, in Fullerton, California; Vera is a school teacher, in Pomona, California; Darnelle teaches high school in Fresno, California; Gena May is positioned in the Veterans Hospital in North Little Rock, Arkansas. Three of the boys are military chaplains: George W. Linzey in the Navy Chaplain Corps, James F. Linzey in the Air Force Chaplaincy, and Paul E. Linzey in the U.S. Army Reserve Chaplaincy. Paul also pastors a church in Encinitas, California.

A Pearl Harbor Victory

As we have stated, in the first few months of the U.S. involvement in World War II, our American forces sank every Japanese ship that participated in the infamous attack on Pearl Harbor. But there was an even more significant victory after the war.

Commander Mitsuo Fuchida was the chief pilot on the Japanese aircraft carrier AKAGI and the leader in the attack on Pearl Harbor. He was the pilot who shouted, "TO RA! TO RA! TO RA!" He would also have flown at the Battle of Midway, but he had been immobilized by an attack of appendicitis and could not fly that day. Judging by what happened to most of his companions, he might not have survived that battle.

After the war, Commander Fuchida had a marvelous conversion experience after reading the New Testament Gospel of Luke and Sgt. Jacob De Shazer's tract, "I Was a Prisoner of Japan." He later lectured in the United States on his spiritual pilgrimage and acceptance of Jesus Christ as his Savior and Lord.

We do not like hardships, trials and testings. We do our best to shun them. But, such are the ironies and paradoxes of war and adversity. Furthermore, good can come of evil if we take adversity in a right spirit, and respond to it in a positive manner.

As I look back on my long career in the U.S. Navy, the blessings of God in giving me a loving and praying wife, His protection from close hits of enemy bombs and torpedoes, and His miraculous deliverance from the sinking of the USS YORKTOWN (CV-5), I praise His holy name and declare that surely God was at Midway.

Bibliography

1. Allen, Thomas B. *National Geographic*: "Pearl Harbor" Washington, D.C.: 1991.
2. Cressman, Robert. *That Gallant Ship USS Yorktown (CV - 5)*. Missoula, Montana: Pictorial Histories Publishing Co., 1985.
3. Holy Bible. (King James Version)
4. Linzey, Stanford E., Jr. *Pentecost in the Pentagon*. New York: Exposition Press, 1975.
5. Lord, Walter. *Incredible Victory*. New York: Harper and Row, Publisher, 1967.
6. Prange, Gordon W. *Miracle at Midway*. New York: Penguin Books, 1982.
7. Stephen, Martin. *Sea Battles in Close-Up: World War II*. Annapolis, Maryland: Naval Institute Press, 1988.
8. *Yorktown Crier*. Lamar, Missouri: USS Yorktown CV-5 Club, Inc., 1983.
9. *Yorktown Crier*. "A Clear Day at Midway". Lamar, Missouri: USS Yorktown CV-5 Club, Inc., 1990.
10. *Yorktown Crier*. 50th Anniversary Edition. USS Yorktown CV-5 Club, Inc., June 4, 1992.

DR. STANFORD E. LINZEY, JR.

Dr. Linzey has traveled throughout the United States, Canada and Mexico ministering The Baptism with the Holy Spirit. His travels have taken him to Europe where he ministered in Spain and Italy. He has toured the Far East repeatedly ministering in Hawaii, Korea, Okinawa, The Philippines, Japan, Singapore and Hong Kong. Over 18,000 people have received the Baptism with the Spirit in the Chaplain's ministry.

Dr. Linzey received the B.A. and Th.B. degrees from the Linda Vista Baptist Bible College and seminary in El Cajon, California, the Master of Divinity from the American Baptist Seminary of the West, Berkeley, California. He studied for one year at Harvard Divinity School as a resident graduate. Fuller Theological Seminary, Pasadena, California, conferred on him the Doctor of Ministry Degree in 1980.

On July 1, 1955, CAPTAIN LINZEY was accepted into the Chaplain Corp, United States Navy, with the rank of Lieutenant Junior Grade. He was promoted to the rank of CAPTAIN, on July 1, 1972. He was the first Assemblies of God Chaplain in the regular Navy and the first Chaplain to attain the rank of CAPTAIN from that church. He retired after 28 years of Naval service in 1974.